Foundation GNVQ
Leisure and Tourism

CW00351239

Foundation GNVQ Leisure and Tourism

Carole Jones

Margaret Radcliffe

Longman

Pearson Education Limited
Edinburgh Gate
Harlow
Essex CM20 2JE, England
and Associated Companies throughout the world

© Pearson Education 2000

The right of Carole Jones and Margaret Radcliffe to be identified as the authors
of this Work has been asserted by them in accordance with the Copyright,
Designs and Patents Act 1988.

All rights reserved; no part of this publication may be reproduced, stored in a
retrieval system, or transmitted in any form or by any means, electronic,
mechanical, photocopying, recording or otherwise without either the prior
written permission of the Publishers or a licence permitting restricted copying in
the United Kingdom issued by the Copyright Licensing Agency Ltd, 90
Tottenham Court Road, London W1P 0LP.

First edition published 1997
This edition published 2000
Second impression 2000

ISBN 0 582 38163 0

British Library Cataloguing-in-Publication Data

A catalogue record for this book is available from the British Library.

Set by 3 in Humanist, Rotis Serif, Caslon

Produced by Pearson Education

Printed in Malaysia, PP

Contents

Acknowledgements

The authors and publishers are grateful to the following for permission to reproduce copyright material:

Calderdale Countryside and Forestry Unit for Figure 1.1

Teversal Trail Visitors' Centre for Figure 1.4

Eureka! The Museum for Children for Figures 1.5, 1.6, 1.17 and 3.4

The Queen's Hotel, Leeds for Figures 1.7, 3.5, 3.8, 3.9 and 3.10

The Stafford Arms, Halifax for Figure 1.8

Halifax Roller Hockey Club for Figures 1.9 and 2.3

Hastings and St Leonards Tourist Board for Figures 1.10, 1.12, 1.16, 1.21 and 2.4

Yorkshire Dales National Park for Figures 1.11 and 1.14

Wirksworth Heritage Centre for Figure 1.13

Eyam Hall 2000 for Figures 1.14 and 2.6

Cartwright Hall Art Gallery and Stable Gallery, Appersett for Figure 1.15

Anglo Canadian Alloys for Figure 2.3

Audit Bureau of Circulations for Figure 2.5

Board of Trustees of the Armouries, Leeds for Figures 2.8 and 2.9

Whilst every effort has been made to trace the owners of copyright material, in a few cases this has proved impossible and we take this opportunity to offer our apologies to any copyright holders whose rights we may have unwittingly infringed.

Throughout this book the following icons are used

Key Words – words that need explaining are highlighted in the text. Each of these key words is explained in the box.

Case Study – these show where we have written about real leisure and tourism facilities.

Exercise – small exercises that are designed to test what you have learned.

Activity – activities that help you to practise what you have learned. Some of the evidence may be used in your portfolio – check with your teacher.

There are three icons that represent the Key Skills:

Communication

Application of number

Information technology

Where you see these icons there will be opportunities for you to practise the Key Skill and you may be able to use the work in your Key Skills portfolio.

Introduction

Welcome to the new edition of the *Foundation GNVQ Leisure and Tourism* textbook.

It has been written to:

- **Give you a broad understanding of leisure and tourism**

- **Develop your skills, knowledge and understanding for the compulsory units**

- **Give you a chance to do practical activities to help you remember what you have learned**

- **Develop your key skills**

What is a GNVQ?

GNVQ stands for General National Vocational Qualification.

- ✪ **General** = broad qualification based around a vocational area; in this book it is the leisure and tourism industries

- ✪ **National** = the qualification is recognised by schools, colleges and employers across the whole country

- ✪ **Vocational** = the qualification is work-related; this book relates to the type of work found in the leisure and tourism industries

- ✪ **Qualification** = you will receive a certificate for this qualification from Edexcel, AQA or OCR that will show and recognise your achievement on this programme at a certain grade (pass, merit or distinction)

What is Foundation level?

GNVQs are at three different levels:

- ✪ **Foundation**

- ✪ **Intermediate**

- ✪ **Vocational A-level**

  - • **Travel and Tourism**

  - • **Leisure and Recreation**

You are studying the Foundation level that is broadly the same as GCSE grades D to G.

Who is the Foundation GNVQ suitable for?

The programme is for pupils or students who:

- ✪ **Are interested in leisure and tourism**

- ✪ **Want to study a subject that relates to their own lives and experiences**

- ✪ **Enjoy coursework and practical work**

- ✪ **Want to study by finding things out for themselves**

- ✪ **Want to learn about different leisure and tourism industries and their customers**

What is the difference between a Full award and a Part One?

A Full award has six different units:

- ✪ **Three compulsory units:** you have no choice and you must study them

- ✪ **Three optional units:** you have to take three units from a list of different units; you, your school or your college can choose which three units to study

Each unit is assessed by *one* method only. Some units are assessed by portfolio (coursework) and others have external assessments (tests). A Full award is worth four GCSE grades.

A Part One has three compulsory units; you have no choice and you must study them. Each unit is assessed by portfolio (coursework) *and* external assessment (test). A Part One is worth two GCSE grades.

What are the compulsory units?

Investigating leisure and tourism

This unit is an introduction to the leisure and tourism industries; you will look at the facilities they offer.

Promotion in leisure and tourism

This unit looks at the different ways that leisure and tourism organisations promote their facilities and services.

Exploring customer service in leisure and tourism

This unit will get you to find out why customer service is so important in leisure and tourism.

If you are taking the Full award:

Remember, if you are taking the Full award, you will do the three compulsory units given above plus three optional units.

Will I get a certificate if I don't finish the whole programme?

Yes, you will get a certificate showing each of the units you have achieved and the grade.

What can I do after finishing the programme?

- ✪ **Get a job and maybe continue to take qualifications such as NVQs**

- ✪ **Take the next level of GNVQ – Intermediate**

- ✪ **Take academic qualifications such as GCSEs and possibly GCE A/AS levels**

What are the six key skills?

- ✪ **Communication**
- ✪ **Application of number**
- ✪ **Information technology**
- ✪ **Working with others**
- ✪ **Improving own learning and performance**
- ✪ **Problem solving**

You do not have to pass the key skills to pass the GNVQ but you may wish to work towards them as you will be using these skills when you produce your portfolio of evidence (coursework).

Key skills units are at five different levels: level 1, level 2, level 3, level 4 and level 5.

Level 1 is the level that you will be expected to achieve if you are taking a Foundation programme but there is nothing to stop you achieving higher levels if you work hard.

If you are at school in Year 10 or 11, you can take the first three key skills units only. If you are older than 16, you can take all six key skills units.

Talk to your teacher to find out whether or not you will be working towards achieving key skills units at your school or college.

The first three key skills are assessed by portfolio (coursework) *and* external assessment (test).

The last three key skills are assessed by portfolio (coursework) at the moment but this may change in the future.

Exercise 0.1

Read the introduction and answer the following questions:

1 What does GNVQ stand for?

2 How many compulsory units do you have to achieve for a Full award? How many for a Part One?

3 a. GNVQ certificates show achievement at three grades; name them.

  P ...   M ....   D ....

  b. GNVQs may be studied at three different levels; name them.

  F ....   I ....   V ....

4 Do you have to study optional units on a Part One programme?

5 Do you have to pass key skills to pass your GNVQ programme?

6 Key skills may be taken at how many levels?

7 How many key skills are there?

8 Name the first three key skills on page 5.

9 What is portfolio evidence? Is it coursework or is it a test?

10 Name one thing you can do after passing your Foundation GNVQ.

Well done, you are now ready to learn about leisure and tourism.

This textbook covers what you need to learn to pass the compulsory units on your GNVQ Foundation Leisure and Tourism programme. It also contains lots of small activities to help you remember what you have learned and to help you begin to collect evidence for your portfolio.

Good luck.

Investigating leisure and tourism

1

In this unit you will find out about:

- **How people spend their leisure** ✓
- **Factors influencing people's choice of leisure activity** ✓
- **Different types of leisure facility** ✓
- **Tourism** ✓
- **Travel** ✓
- **Travel and tourism in your chosen area** ✓
- **Information sources** ✓

How people spend their leisure

Most people will spend a large part of each day either at school, college, work or asleep. The rest of the time people are generally free to choose what they want to do. This is their leisure time.

Some people like to do active things (e.g. playing football) and others prefer passive activities (e.g. watching videos).

Everyone likes to spend their leisure time doing different things and there are lots of leisure activities to choose from:

- ✪ **Reading**

- ✪ **Sport (joining in or watching)**

- ✪ **Going to the cinema or theatre**

- ✪ **Going for a walk**

- ✪ **Watching television or listening to the radio**

- ✪ **Eating out**

- ✪ **Playing computer games**

- ✪ **Visiting a tourist attraction**

Exercise 1.1

For each of the above types of leisure activity, state whether it is active or passive.

Reading

Reading has always been a popular leisure activity with people of all ages. There are many types of reading material, including magazines, books, newspapers and comics. Recent surveys show that reading tends to be more popular with women than men.

Schools now have reading and literacy weeks where local business people, parents and other volunteers can visit the school to help encourage pupils to read more.

Sport

Sport is one of the biggest areas of the leisure industry. Many people enjoy taking part in different sporting activities (known as participating or joining in).

But remember that many people prefer to watch the activities rather than take part – they are spectating. Here are two examples:

- ✪ **Going to watch a major football match**

- ✪ **Watching an athletics competition**

Circle the 10 different sports hidden in the following wordsearch. We have circled one of them for you.

Football Hockey   Swimming   Golf   Canoeing
Skating   Diving   Cycling   Fishing   Squash

C	Y	C	L	I	N	G	A	B	L	C
L	A	E	B	O	X	I	C	S	L	Y
D	G	N	I	R	P	L	G	G	A	E
M	G	S	O	I	B	A	R	B	B	K
B	D	E	G	E	F	G	B	H	T	C
H	J	D	K	N	I	R	L	M	O	O
N	F	I	S	H	I	N	G	R	O	H
Z	N	V	O	L	P	M	G	Q	F	S
S	P	I	O	F	T	U	M	V	W	A
X	O	N	W	L	Z	A	B	I	C	U
D	G	G	E	O	F	G	H	I	W	Q
J	W	K	L	G	N	I	T	A	K	S

Activity

1.1

1   In groups of three, produce an alphabet of sports. For example, A = archery, B = basketball. How many did you manage to do?

2   a. List the sports that you like to play and the ones you like to watch.

b. Discuss your lists with others in the group.

Going to the cinema or theatre

Most towns and cities will have at least one cinema and many also have theatres (e.g. the White Rock Theatre in Hastings).

Theatres are places where people go to see different types of live entertainment (e.g. concerts, plays, musicals and comedy shows). Some theatres are used by local amateur groups as well as professional companies.

Even though many people rent videos to watch at home, cinemas are increasingly popular places for people to spend their leisure time. As well as cinemas that are located in town centres, there are now many multi-screen cinemas situated on the outskirts of towns (e.g. Showcase Cinemas and UCI).

Multi-screen cinemas tend to be more expensive but people like them because they have large car parks, comfortable seating and a wide range of films to choose from.

Activity 1.2

1   Look in your local newspaper and find some advertisements for theatres and cinemas.

2   List 10 films and performances that are currently on offer.

3   Choose three that interest you and say why.

Going for a walk

Many people take regular walks each day as part of their normal routine. They may:

- ✪ **Walk to work, school or college**

- ✪ **Take their dog for a walk**

- ✪ **Take their children to the local park or walk them to school**

▼ ▼ ▼ ▼ ▼ ▼ ▼ ▼
Physical
activity that involves
using your body and
needs quite a lot of
energy
▲ ▲ ▲ ▲ ▲ ▲ ▲ ▲

Walking regularly features in the top 10 sports, games and **physical** activities for men and women; in a recent survey 45 per cent of adults said they had been for a walk of 2 miles (3.2 km) or more in the last four weeks. Walking is a free activity that anyone, of any age, can do.

Tourist information centres often sell leaflets showing popular routes for walking in their area. There are also many books that have been written to help people choose suitable walks that give details on the length and difficulty of the walk (e.g. the *Walker's Companion* series published by Ward Lock and *Great Walks in the Peak District* by John and Anne Nuttall).

Figure 1.1 shows a walk taken from the 'Walks Around the Villages' leaflets produced by Calderdale Countryside and Forestry Unit.

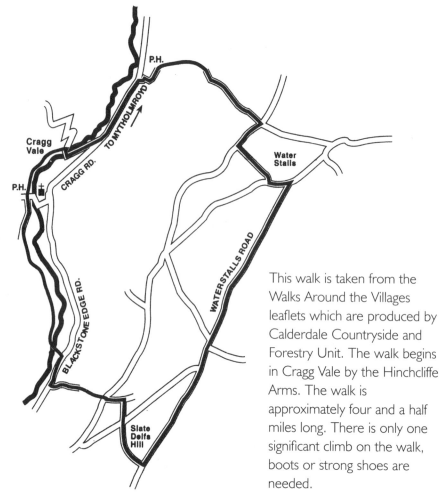

This walk is taken from the Walks Around the Villages leaflets which are produced by Calderdale Countryside and Forestry Unit. The walk begins in Cragg Vale by the Hinchcliffe Arms. The walk is approximately four and a half miles long. There is only one significant climb on the walk, boots or strong shoes are needed.

Figure 1.1 *Calderdale council publishes routes for walkers*
Courtesy Calderdale Countryside and Forestry Unit

Activity 1.3

1   Answer the following questions:

a.   Approximately how many miles is this walk?

b.   Assume an average person walks at 3 miles per hour. How long would it take the average person to complete the walk?

2   Find some information about walks on offer in your area and make a leaflet giving details about them.

Watching television or listening to the radio

Watching television and listening to the radio are still extremely popular ways that people spend their leisure time.

Surveys state that over 95 per cent of people watch television regularly and over 85 per cent listen to the radio. Videos have made television even more popular as people often record programmes they are unable to watch at the time, or they rent and buy videos. Satellite and cable television have also led to an increase in the amount of time people spend watching television programmes.

Activity 1.4

1   Find out from each member of your group how long they watched television for last night (to the nearest hour) and the names of the programmes they watched.
2   Which was the most popular programme?
3   Calculate the average time spent watching the television.

Eating out

Public houses
places that are licensed to sell alcohol to people over 18, who often go there to meet friends (usually called pubs)

You need only look in your own town at the number and variety of eating places to see the popularity of eating out. Most **public houses** now provide food as well as drink, and there are a wide range of restaurants selling different types of food (e.g. Indian, Chinese, Mexican, Greek and more traditional food such as fish and chips). Figure 1.2 shows Pizza Hut in Halifax displaying some special offers (e.g. pizza for £2.00 and a no-limits buffet for £3.49).

Figure 1.2 *Pizza Hut posters display special offers*

Activity 1.5

Look in a business telephone directory, such as Yellow Pages, under restaurants. Find as many different types as you can and list them with an example. We have given you two to help you:

Type of restaurant	Example
Italian	Al Mulinos
Indian	Akbars

Playing computer games

Computer games are now more popular than ever before. There are amusement arcades in towns, leisure facilities and motorway service stations where people can go to play computer games.

Many households now have their own games consoles and/or personal computers, giving them access to an endless range of computer games. Many national newspapers, magazines and websites have sections describing new computer games.

Activity
1.6

1   Do you play computer games?
2   What types of game do you play?
3   What do you like about them?
4   Choose one game and write a short article about it that you hope will encourage others to try out the game.

Visiting a tourist attraction

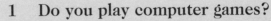

Tourist attractions can be man-made (e.g. Alton Towers) or natural (e.g. Lake Windermere).

There are three main types of tourist attraction in the United Kingdom:

✪ **Recreational:** national parks, tourist resorts, etc.

✪ **Cultural and entertainment:** heritage sites, galleries, theatres, etc.

✪ **Children's attractions:** theme parks, zoos, museums, farms, leisure pools, etc.

We will be covering these attractions in more depth later in this unit. However, it is important to realise that there are a wide range to choose from. Visits to these attractions may last from an hour to several days.

Exercise 1.3

1   List three man-made tourist attractions.
2   List three natural tourist attractions.

Other activities

We have given you some examples of the ways that people like to spend their leisure time but there are many more, including:

- ✪ **Do-it-yourself (DIY)**
- ✪ **Fishing**
- ✪ **Trainspotting**
- ✪ **Shopping**
- ✪ **Playing cards**
- ✪ **Painting and sketching**
- ✪ **Birdwatching**
- ✪ **Sunbathing**
- ✪ **Having barbecues and picnics**
- ✪ **Operating radio-controlled trains, boats and cars**
- ✪ **Taking photographs**
- ✪ **Metal detecting**
- ✪ **Collecting rocks and fossils**
- ✪ **Gardening**

The list is endless. Can you think of five more?

1   Calculate how much leisure time you had last week.

2   List all the different ways you used your leisure time during that week and approximately how much time you spent on each type of activity.

3   Produce a pie chart that shows your leisure activities for that week.

4   Look at your pie chart and list your three most popular leisure activities.

5   Share your findings with others in your group and produce a graph to show the most popular activities.

Some of these leisure activities are known as home-based leisure, for example:

✪ **Reading**

✪ **Watching television**

✪ **Computer games**

Home-based leisure is growing every year as people tend to spend more and more of their leisure time taking part in activities at home.

Exercise 1.4

Look at the pie chart you produced for the last activity. What percentage of your activities are home-based?

Factors influencing people's choice of leisure activity

Many things can affect the way people spend their leisure time. These include their:

✪ **Age group**

✪ **Culture**

✪ **Special needs**

✪ **Household set-up**

  • **families**

  • **single people**

  • **couples**

✪ **Gender (male or female)**

Age group

Senior citizens
someone who is entitled to draw a state retirement pension

The different ways that people spend their leisure time may depend on their age. Here are some examples of how teenagers and **senior citizens** might spend their leisure time:

✪ **Senior citizens often like to take off-season holidays**

✪ **Teenagers like to visit theme parks**

Off-season holidays are taken in the least popular months such as May and October.

Activity
1.8

Think of two different ways that the following age groups may like to spend their leisure time and complete the table.

	Toddlers (age 1–4)	Under 12s	Teenagers	Adults	Senior citizens
Activity 1					
Activity 2					

Culture

Tradition and culture can affect the way people spend their leisure time. Certain cultures are more family-oriented and like to eat out with their children whereas others may prefer to spend time with adults.

Special needs

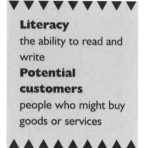

Literacy
the ability to read and write

Potential customers
people who might buy goods or services

There are a wide range of special needs that people may have, such as visual needs, **literacy** needs, wheelchair needs; these can restrict access to certain types of leisure activities. However, many facilities try to ensure they meet as many needs as possible of all their **potential customers**. Most facilities display the following symbol to show they provide facilities for disabled users.

Figure 1.3 *People with disabilities look for this sign*

If you want to encourage visitors who cannot speak or read much English, your leaflet needs to be in different languages or it must include lots of photographs, diagrams and symbols.

Teversal Trail Visitors' Centre uses symbols to let people know about the facilities available. The leaflet also includes photographs and maps that are fairly easy to understand.

FACILITIES

P	Ample free car parking	i	Information
♿	Wheelchair access to the Centre, toilets and parts of the trails		Suitable for school parties
	Public conveniences	🚲	Cycle hire facilities
	Refreshments and hot snacks for sale	🦋	Ideal for nature study
	Souvenirs for sale		Reference books and spotter sheets available for public use

Figure 1.4 *Teversal Trail uses these symbols for its facilities*
Courtesy Teversal Trail Visitors' Centre

▼▼▼▼▼▼▼▼▼
Facility
the building, area or
place offering the
goods and services
▲▲▲▲▲▲▲▲▲

1   Think of a leisure facility that you often visit. List anything that you feel has been provided to meet customers' special needs and requirements (e.g. ramp access for wheelchairs).

2   Is there anything missing that you feel should be provided for customers with special needs? Give your reasons.

Household set-up

A person may live alone, in a couple or in a family, and their household set-up will change as their personal circumstances change (e.g. if they have a baby or their children leave home).

However, someone who is married with children might not always take part in leisure activities that are designed for families. They may:

✪ **Want to spend some time away from their family with friends**

✪ **Have a night out with their partner**

✪ **Go away for a short break without their children**

Robert is 42 years old and married. He has two daughters, one aged 9 years and another aged 6 months. His wife, Judith, is 38. Here are some examples of the way Robert spends his leisure time:

★ Once a week he plays football with his work **colleagues**

★ Twice a week he plays table tennis with friends

★ Once a month he goes out with Judith for a meal

★ Every weekend he and Judith take the children to the local park

★ Every year they visit America for their family holiday

★ When the grandparents take the children on holiday, Judith and Robert visit a **health farm** for a luxury break

Although Robert falls into the category of 'family', he does not spend all his leisure time with them. For each of the above examples, decide whether Robert is taking part in them as a single person, part of a couple or part of a family.

Colleagues
people that you work with

Health farm
type of hotel that provides special diets, treatments and exercise programmes

Gender

Your gender, male or female, may influence the way you choose to spend your leisure time. However, it is becoming less important than it was in the past, when women found it more difficult to take part in some activities. There are, however, still some examples where your gender can affect your choice. For example, some private golf clubs still do not allow women to become full members, and boxing is still mainly a male sport.

Other factors

Other things can influence how people spend their leisure time:

- ✪ **Availability of local facilities**
- ✪ **Availability of transport**
- ✪ **People's interests**
- ✪ **Fashion**
- ✪ **Influence of family and friends**
- ✪ **Money to spend on leisure**

Availability of local facilities

If you live in a large city there will be lots of different ways that you can spend your leisure time. If you live in the countryside there may be less choice.

Activity 1.11

1   In small groups, choose a city and a rural village.
2   Find out what leisure activities are available in each area for teenagers.
3   Compare and discuss your findings with other groups.

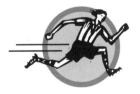

Availability of transport

Some activities do not require any transport at all (e.g. watching television and reading). Others may require transport in order to get there (e.g. going to a cinema).

Many people have access to cars but others rely on public transport (e.g. trains and buses), cycling and taxis.

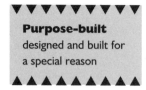

Purpose-built
designed and built for
a special reason

Most **purpose-built** attractions will need to be located close to motorways or railway stations, or they should be on a bus route to ensure that visitors can get to them easily.

The photograph below shows Eureka! The Museum for Children; it is situated next to Halifax railway station, which has direct rail connections to York, Leeds, Bradford, Manchester and Blackpool.

Figure 1.5 *Eureka! is situated next to Halifax railway station*
Courtesy Eureka! The Museum for Children

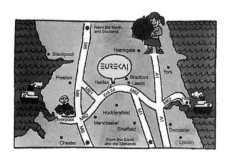

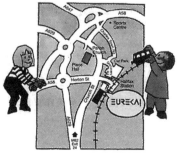

Eureka! is a short walk from Halifax bus station, with buses running daily from Leeds, Bradford, Huddersfield, Wakefield, Keighley, Dewsbury, Rochdale, Oldham and Burnley. It is approximately 5 miles (8 km) from junction 24 on the M62. It has its own car park area.

Figure 1.6 *Two clearly drawn maps show Eureka!'s location*
Courtesy Eureka! The Museum for Children

To find out more, you can contact Eureka by:

- ✪ **Post: Discovery Road, Halifax, West Yorkshire HX1 2NE**
- ✪ **Telephone: 01422 330012**
- ✪ **Information line: 01426 983191 (24 hours)**
- ✪ **Fax: 01422 330275**
- ✪ **Homepage: www.eureka.org.uk**

▼▼▼▼▼▼▼▼▼
Brochures
leaflets that give
details about goods or
services
▲▲▲▲▲▲▲▲▲

Figure 1.7 shows a 'How to find us' section from a brochure produced by the Queen's Hotel in Leeds; it should help you with the following activity. You may also find it helpful to collect some **brochures** on different types of leisure facilities to see what information they include.

HOW TO FIND US:

By Rail
The Queen's Hotel is conveniently adjacent to Leeds Railway Station.

By Air
The Queen's Hotel is only 12 miles from Leeds Airport, along the A65.

By Road
FROM THE SOUTH
M621, (M1 & M62) Motorways: follow the signs to Leeds City Centre, along Neville Street, towards City Square. After the traffic lights, take a left into the slip road, in front of The Queen's Hotel.

FROM THE NORTH EAST
Take main A road into Leeds, then follow City Centre Loop to Junction One. After the traffic lights, take a left into the slip road, in front of The Queen's Hotel.

FROM THE NORTH WEST
Leave the Inner Ring Road at Westgate. Drive along Westgate and turn right along Park Row, keeping in the right hand lane. At the end of Park Row, drive across the main road into the slip road in front of The Queen's Hotel.

FOR RESIDENTS
As you turn into The Queen's, park outside the Hotel and our Car Jockey Porters will park your car.

FOR NON RESIDENTS
We recommend the Railway Station Car Park in Aire Street.

By Coach
Ten minutes walk from the National Coach Station.

Figure 1.7 *The Queen's Hotel in Leeds tells guests how to find it*
Courtesy the Queen's Hotel, Leeds

Activity 1.12

1   Choose a local leisure facility.
2   Design a section called 'How to find us' for your chosen facility that can be used in a new brochure.

People's interests

People tend to spend their leisure time doing things that they enjoy and are interested in. Here are two examples:

✪ **Peter is interested in art:** in his leisure time he visits galleries and reads books about artists and their lives

✪ **Rhona is interested in Manchester United:** she visits Old Trafford regularly and buys football magazines and souvenirs

Exercise 1.5

1 Think of all the different things you are interested in and list them.
2 For each example, write down what you do because of this interest.

Fashion

If you look back over time, you will be able to spot how fads and fashion have influenced people's leisure activities. Here are some examples to help you:

✪ **Paintball clubs:** a few years ago there seemed to be a lot of paintball clubs opening where people could go and play survival games and shoot each other with paint. Some of these clubs have now closed as people have become tired of them and want new things to do

✪ **Tenpin bowling:** Tenpin bowling clubs were very popular in the late 1960s. After a while, many of them closed due to lack of interest. They are now becoming popular again and most towns have a tenpin bowling alley nearby

✪ **Eating and exercise:** in recent years, healthy eating and

Health clubs
places that offer
beauty and health
treatments, exercise
classes and equipment

regular exercise have become very fashionable. This has led to the opening of a large number of **health clubs** and gyms

Family and friends

Most people want to spend their leisure time with family and friends. This can mean they will do things they would not have thought about doing on their own.

Activity 1.13

1 Think of three things you have done with your family or your friends in the last few months, things that you may not have chosen to do on your own.

2 Can you think of something you wanted to do where you had to influence your family or friends to go along with you?

Money to spend on leisure

Money is a major influence on how people fill their leisure time. The amount of money people can spend on leisure activities varies a great deal. Some activities are free (e.g. walking) whereas others cost a lot of money (e.g. flying lessons).

Activity 1.14

1 Calculate the amount of money you have each week to spend on leisure activities.

2 List how you spend this money.

3 If money were not a problem to you – you could afford to do anything – name two leisure activities you would choose.

Different types of leisure facility

The leisure industry includes a wide range of facilities. Here are some typical facilities that might be found in your area:

- ✪ **Leisure centres and health clubs**
- ✪ **Libraries**
- ✪ **Video rental shops**
- ✪ **Cinemas**
- ✪ **Pubs, restaurants and takeaway restaurants**
- ✪ **Community centres**
- ✪ **Clubs**
- ✪ **Sports venues**
- ✪ **Theme parks**
- ✪ **Home-based leisure**

Leisure centres and health clubs

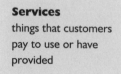

Services
things that customers pay to use or have provided

Most towns have a leisure centre that offers a wide range of **services** and activities (e.g. badminton courts, swimming lessons, fitness rooms and aerobics). They are often owned by the local authority, which tries to provide services at a reasonable price that encourages local people to take part in healthy activities.

Many towns also have at least one health club. Health clubs are usually privately owned and tend to provide a range of equipment for weight and fitness training. They may also provide a range of classes (e.g. aerobics and circuit training) and sometimes they have small swimming pools, saunas and steam rooms.

Libraries

All local authorities provide at least one library in their area. Everyone who lives close by can join their library, free of charge, to use the services. Libraries now provide a wide range of services, some of them free and others for a small charge. These services include:

❂ **Book loans**

❂ **Video rental**

❂ **CD and tape rental**

❂ **Reference facilities**

❂ **Children's activities**

❂ **Internet facilities**

Schools, colleges and universities also have libraries for their students. Quite often universities will allow members of the public to use their library facilities, but they may make a small charge.

Activity 1.15

1 Visit your local library. What other services does your library provide, apart from loaning books?

2 What do these extra services cost?

3 Produce an A4 poster that could be used to advertise your local library.

Video rental shops

In 1982 less than 20 per cent of households owned a video recorder. The number now is above 80 per cent; this has led to a large increase in the number of video rental shops over the past 20 years. Video rental shops range from large multinational chains (e.g. Blockbuster) to small corner shops providing video rental as an extra service.

Cinemas

Many people spend part of their leisure time at the cinema watching films and socialising with their friends and family. The range of films on offer varies depending on the size of the cinema. Some local cinemas may only offer one film whereas large multiplexes may offer up to 12 films at any one time.

Activity 1.16

1 Find an advertisement for a large cinema complex (e.g. Showcase Cinema) and write down all the films on offer this week.

2 Survey at least 50 students at your school or college and produce a graph to show the popularity of each film (you may wish to do this in small groups).

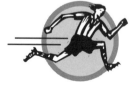

Pubs, restaurants and takeaway restaurants

Eating out is a popular way of spending leisure time and there is a huge choice of places to eat.

The majority of pubs now provide some kind of food for customers. This can range from sandwiches through to three-course meals with restaurant service. The Stafford Arms offers the menu, shown in Figure 1.8.

We have already looked at the different types of restaurants and the kind of food provided by them. However, takeaway restaurants are becoming increasingly popular with all ages due to the increase in home-based leisure activities. Quite often people will rent a video to watch at home and order a takeaway as a treat.

STAFFORD ARMS

LITE BITES

SOUP
Served with roll & butter
£1.50

GARLIC MUSHROOMS
Coated in crispy breadcrumb served with garlic mayonnaise dip
£2.25

GARLIC BREAD
Topped with melted cheese
£1.75

VEGETABLE SPRING ROLLS
Served with sweet & sour sauce
£2.25

FISH CAKES
Coated in breadcrumbs served with tartare sauce
£2.25

GIANT YORKSHIRE PUDDINGS
Served with a choice of fillings

ONION GRAVY
£1.75
Can be served as a lite bite

CUMBERLAND SAUSAGE
£2.50

ROAST BEEF
£3.25

CHILLI CON CARNE
£2.50

JACKET POTATOES
Served with a choice of fillings & crisp salad garnish

CHILLI CON CARNE	£2.50	CHEESE	£2.25
TUNA & MAYONNAISE	£2.25	CHICKEN CURRY	£2.75
BAKED BEANS	£1.95	COLESLAW	£1.95
PLAIN WITH BUTTER	£1.75		

Figure 1.8 *The Stafford Arms serves giant Yorkshire puddings*
Courtesy the Stafford Arms

Community centres

Most towns have several types of community centre, each offering a range of services and facilities.

Some community centres offer general services that would interest a wide range of people. Others focus on special groups of people, for example:

✪ **Asian Women's and Girls' Centre**

✪ **Christian Family Centre**

✪ **Residents' Association**

Activity 1.17

1   Using a local telephone directory, find out the names of five different community centres in your area.

2   Choose two community centres and either visit or telephone them to find out what they offer and for whom.

Clubs

Clubs cover a huge range of activities. There are flying clubs, chess clubs, line dancing clubs, youth clubs, Scout and Guide groups, and social clubs; the list is endless.

Figure 1.9 shows the cover of a leaflet used by Halifax Roller Hockey Club. Inside it explains:

✪ **What roller hockey is**

✪ **When it started**

HALIFAX ROLLER HOCKEY CLUB

TIRED OF SKATING IN CIRCLES ???

TIRED OF HAVING TO SKATE SLOWLY ???

WANT TO TRY SOMETHING NEW ???

EVER THOUGHT OF ROLLER HOCKEY ???

TURN OVER TO FIND OUT MORE !

Figure 1.9 *A leaflet's first page aims to make you read more*
Courtesy Halifax Roller Hockey Club

✪ **How much it costs to play**

✪ **The name, address and telephone number of key contacts**

It also includes an application form to complete if you want to join.

Many clubs are run by volunteers who do not get any pay for doing the work. Peter Radcliffe is the treasurer for Halifax Roller Hockey Club. He is a volunteer and does not receive any payment for this role. As treasurer he:

✪ **Collects money each week from the players**

✪ **Orders equipment**

✪ **Banks money and keeps accounts**

✪ **Goes to meetings to discuss the club**

✪ **Produces a report for the annual general meeting (AGM)**

✪ **Helps out with various other tasks, such as giving players a lift to away matches**

Activity 1.18

1   In pairs, find out about a club in your area. If possible, interview a leading member of the club.

2   Give your group a 5 minute oral presentation that answers these questions:

   a. What type of club is it?
   b. How long has it been going?
   c. How many members does it have?
   d. How much does it cost to join?
   e. What activities and services does it offer its members?

   You can add to this list if you want to.

3   Produce a display with others in your group showing a range of clubs in your area.

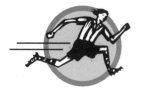

Sports venues

Sports venues are places where sport takes place. They can vary in their size and the facilities they offer. Wembley Stadium can hold thousands of spectators who pay to watch professional matches; a local football ground may hold only a small number of people. Here are some sporting venues:

✪ **Swimming pools**

✪ **Football grounds**

- ✪ **Athletics arenas**
- ✪ **Rugby grounds**
- ✪ **Racecourses**

Exercise 1.6

Match the events on the left with the venues on the right.

Cricket test match	White Hart Lane
University boat race	Aintree
The Grand National	Lords
Athletics meeting	Twickenham
FA Cup Final	Crystal Palace
The All England Championships	St Andrews
Golf tournament	Wembley
Motor racing	The Thames
Football	Silverstone
Rugby	Wimbledon

Theme parks

Theme parks are one of the major leisure attractions in the United Kingdom. Most theme parks are open only during certain months of the year. Visitors usually pay an entrance fee that allows unlimited access to all the rides.

1   Match the theme parks on the left with the counties on the right. We have completed one of them for you.

Drayton Manor	Lancashire
Brean Leisure Park	Surrey
Flamingo Land	Surrey
Lightwater Valley	Staffordshire
Thorpe Park	Tyne and Wear
Alton Towers	North Yorkshire
Chessington World of Adventure	Staffordshire
Metroland	Derbyshire
American Adventure	Somerset
Camelot	North Yorkshire
Legoland	Berkshire

2   Choose one of the theme parks from those given above. Find out as much as you can about it. You could do this by:

 a. Collecting information leaflets
 b. Visiting the park
 c. Contacting the park
 d. Using the Internet

3   Write a small report detailing:

 a. Where you can get food and the type of food on offer
 b. Any services provided for customers with special needs
 c. Other services on offer (e.g. shops and baby changing)

Visitors need to be careful when choosing which theme park to visit as some have only a limited amount of rides for young children whereas others have lots of gentle rides that are more suitable.

Home-based leisure

Because of the increasing popularity of home-based leisure, more and more facilities have to provide services to meet this need. These include:

✪ **Takeaway restaurants**

✪ **Video rental shops**

✪ **Book shops**

✪ **Shops selling computer games**

Tourism

▼▼▼▼▼▼▼▼▼
Tourists
people who are visiting an area in their leisure time
▲▲▲▲▲▲▲▲▲

Tourism involves travel away from home or work. Some **tourists** make short visits whereas others may stay much longer. However, all tourists are expected to return home at some stage.

Many people spend a considerable amount of their leisure time visiting places as tourists. The reasons for the visits could be to:

✪ **Have a holiday**

✪ **Do some sightseeing**

✪ **Visit a tourist attraction**

✪ **Visit friends or relatives**

✪ **Go to a sports event as a spectator or to participate**

Holidays

Holidays can be long or short, ranging from one night to over three weeks. Different people like to take different types of holiday. Some want to go abroad and sunbathe, some prefer to go to UK resorts and visit the local attractions, and some want to visit places far away to experience a different culture.

The majority of holidaymakers will, however, visit a recognised holiday resort of some kind, either in this country or abroad. One of the most visited holiday resorts in Britain is Blackpool.

A good example of a holiday resort in Britain is Hastings and St Leonards. It offers visitors a variety of attractions, known as products; have a look at the products in Figure 1.10.

Activity 1.20

1 Find out the name of five popular holiday resorts in the UK and five holiday resorts abroad.

2 Select one holiday resort from your list that interests you and list its visitor attractions.

3 Select one of your listed attractions and write a short paragraph that describes what it offers to holidaymakers.

Figure 1.10 *Hastings has a castle, a cave, a theatre and a gallery*
Courtesy Hastings and St Leonards Tourist Board

Before deciding whether to visit an area, it is a good idea to look at the attractions on offer to make sure there is something that interests you. Tourist information offices, travel agents and brochures can often give you this information.

Sightseeing

Tourists usually like to spend some of their holiday sightseeing. This may involve visiting interesting buildings, historical sites or areas of outstanding beauty.

Visiting a tourist attraction

There are three major types of visitor attraction in the United Kingdom:

✪ **Recreational attractions**

✪ **Culture and entertainment**

✪ **Children's attractions**

Recreational attractions

National parks

A national park is an area of outstanding natural beauty. A lot of the land in the parks belongs to farmers and landowners, so it is not public property. Public property means that the general public (you and I) can use it freely.

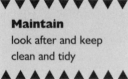

Maintain
look after and keep clean and tidy

Most of the money needed to **maintain** the parks comes from the government and the rest comes from things like entry fees, parking and charges for goods and services.

Here are some of the national parks in England and Wales:

✪ **Brecon Beacons (Tel: 01874 624437)**

✪ **Dartmoor (Tel: 01626 832093)**

✪ **Exmoor (Tel: 01398 323665)**

The Yorkshire Dales National Park

Figure 1.11   *The Yorkshire Dales National Park*
Courtesy Yorkshire Dales National Park

The Yorkshire Dales National Park was established in 1954 and was the seventh national park to be designated. It covers 680 square miles (1,760 km^2), and is the third largest park, only the Lake District and Snowdonia national parks are larger.

Approximately one-eighth of the park is in Cumbria and the rest is in North Yorkshire. The emblem (logo) for the park is the head of a ram.

There are approximately 18,000 people living within the area of the park, 99 per cent of which is owned by farmers and landowners; less than 1 per cent of the park is publicly owned.

Over 8 million people visit the national park each year but 90 per cent of them stay for less than 6 hours.

✪ **Lake District (Tel: 01539 724555)**

✪ **North York Moors (Tel: 01439 770657)**

✪ **Peak District (Tel: 01629 816200)**

✪ **Snowdonia (Tel: 01766 770274)**

✪ **Yorkshire Dales (Tel: 01969 650456)**

1   With the help of your teacher, locate the above national parks on a map of the UK.

2   Choose one of the national parks and obtain a map that shows the area covered by the park.

3   Find out:
a. The year when the park was first **established**
b. The facilities the park offers to tourists
You may find it helpful to use the British Tourist Authority (BTA) website.

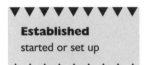

Established
started or set up

Tourist resorts

There are too many different tourist resorts for us to list in this book. A tourist resort is a place that attracts a large number of visitors because it has lots of interesting places to visit and things to do. You have already done an activity listing some of the tourist resorts in this country and abroad.

Figure 1.12 shows a map of Hastings and St Leonards. Hastings has been a fishing port for centuries and the fishing quarter is one of the most fascinating parts of the town. In addition, there is a quaint and picturesque 'old town' with narrow winding streets and Tudor houses.

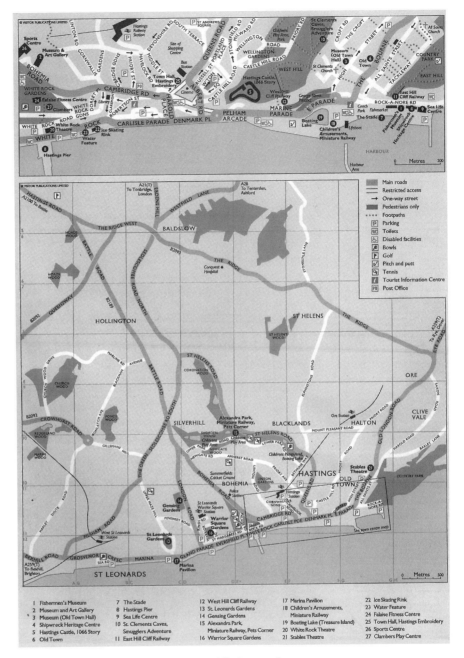

Figure 1.12 *Map of Hastings and St Leonards*
Courtesy Hastings and St Leonards Tourist Board

Hastings is a glorious seaside town but also has plenty of greenery, parkland and wooded areas. St Leonards is next to Hastings; it is a new town with elegant squares and beautiful gardens.

Activity 1.22

Look at the map of Hastings and answer the following questions:

1 How many woods are shown on the map?
2 Name the four railway stations shown on the map.
3 Give the map reference for the Stables Theatre.
4 How many car parks are shown on the map?

Culture and entertainment

Culture and entertainment attractions include:

✪ **Heritage sites**

✪ **Galleries**

✪ **Theatres**

Here are the top 10 museums and galleries and the top 10 historic houses and monuments plus the numbers of people who visited them in 1998. The information is taken from the British Tourist Authority figures for 1998.

Top 10 museums and galleries

1	British Museum, London	5,620,081
2	National Gallery, London	4,770,330
3	Tate Gallery, London	2,180,665
4	National History Museum, London	1,904,539

5	Science Museum, London	1,599,817
6	Glasgow Art Gallery and Museum	1,128,455
7	Victoria and Albert Museum, London	1,110,000
8	National Portrait Gallery, London	1,017,265
9	Royal Academy, London	912,714
10	Birmingham Museum and Art Gallery	828,250

Top 10 historic houses and monuments

1	Tower of London	2,551,459
2	Windsor Castle, Berkshire	1,495,465
3	Edinburgh Castle	1,219,055
4	Roman Baths and Pump Room, Bath	905,426
5	Stonehenge, Wiltshire	817,493
6	Warwick Castle	777,500
7	Hampton Court Palace, London	605,230
8	Leeds Castle, Kent	551,377
9	Shakespeare's Birthplace, Stratford	520,108
10	Chatsworth House, Derbyshire	475,000

Heritage sites

Heritage sites include churches, museums, castles, houses and areas of historical interest. Figure 1.13 shows some examples, and here is a list of some heritage attractions in the UK:

Figure 1.13 *Heritage sites: Bolton, Skipton and Wirksworth*
Wirksworth leaflet courtesy Wirksworth Heritage Centre

Beamish Hall

Bradford Industrial Museum

Bushmead Priory

Captain Cook Memorial Museum

Carisbrooke Castle

Conwy Castle

Cragside House and Gardens

Dartmouth Castle

Ffestiniog Railway

Giant's Causeway

Glastonbury Abbey

Jorvik Viking Centre

Kew Palace

Kirby Hall

Knaresborough Castle

London Transport Museum

Norwich Cathedral

Port Sunlight Heritage Centre

Stonehenge

Tower Museum, Derry

Wroxeter Roman City

York Minster

Figure 1.14 *Historic buildings: Eyam Hall and Bolton Abbey*
Copyright Eyam Hall 2000 and Yorkshire Dales National Park

Activity 1.23

1   Form a group of three or four people then get a map of the UK.

2   Each member of the group should select one of the heritage attractions listed on page 48 and mark its **location** on the map.

3   Find out the opening times and admission prices for each chosen attraction.

4   Produce a small display showing all the information your group has collected.

▼▼▼▼▼▼▼▼▼
Location
place or position
▲▲▲▲▲▲▲▲▲

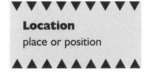

Galleries

Galleries display works of art (e.g. paintings). Figure 1.15 shows two examples, and here are the names and addresses of some galleries in England and Wales:

Figure 1.15 *Picture galleries in Bradford and Hawes*
Courtesy Cartwright Hall Art Gallery and Stable Gallery, Appersett

The National Gallery,
Trafalgar Square,
London WC2N 5DN

Derby Museum Art Gallery,
The Strand,
Derby DE1 1BS

Impressions Gallery,
29 Castlegate,
York YO1 1RN

Laing Art Gallery,
Higham Place,
Newcastle upon Tyne
NE1 8AG

Huddersfield Art Gallery,
Princess Alexandra Walk,
Huddersfield HD1 2SU

Victoria Art Gallery,
Poulteney Bridge,
Bath BA2 4AT

Graham Sutherland Gallery,
Picton Castle,
The Rhos,
Haverfordwest SA62 4AS

Activity 1.24

Besides the examples given above, there are many small, local galleries throughout the UK (and some libraries house art exhibitions).

1 Write down the name and address of a gallery in your locality.

2 Do visitors have to pay to get in?

Theatres

We have already mentioned that most towns will have at least one theatre and we've looked at the types of entertainment they offer. Figure 1.16 shows the White Rock Theatre in Hastings.

Large cities will often have more than one theatre. London has many theatres offering customers a variety of choice.

● WHITE ROCK THEATRE

Hastings' premier entertainment centre, where you can see top class acts all year round. Pop, rock and jazz artistes, top comics and actors, national orchestras and international ballet companies - they all play at the White Rock Theatre! And if you visit Hastings around Christmas, be sure to take the kids to the traditional pantomime, starring some very well known TV faces!

Figure 1.16 *The White Rock Theatre in Hastings*
Courtesy Hastings and St Leonards Tourist Board

Activity 1.25

1   Look in a national newspaper such as the *Times* or the *Guardian*.
2   How many different theatres can you find in London?
3   Name four shows currently on offer.

Children's attractions

Theme parks are a major children's attraction. However, there are many others, including:

- ✪ **Zoos**

- ✪ **Children's museums**

- ✪ **Children's farms and open farms**

- ✪ **Leisure pools**

- ✪ **Play facilities**

Eureka! The Museum for Children

Eureka! The Museum for Children is Britain's first hands-on museum designed especially for children. The winner of 15 major awards, including the English Tourist Board Visitor Attraction of the Year, it has already welcomed over 1.5 million people in its first three years since opening.

Eureka! has four main exhibition areas on two floors of a purpose-built building:

continued

continued

Figure 1.17 *Children discover things at Eureka!*
Courtesy Eureka! The Museum for Children

★ Me and My Body
★ Living and Working Together
★ Invent, Create, Communicate
★ Things

Here children are encouraged to discover for themselves about their bodies and senses, the world around them and the world of communications. They can look and listen, touch and smell, sharing their discoveries with the adults; and even the adults might be amazed at what they find out from over 400 interactive exhibits.

Eureka! has floor staff, called enablers, to help people book in, play with the exhibits and make the most of their visit. Although designed for children up to the age of 12, the museum is suitable for everyone, including people with disabilities and special needs. The entire site is accessible to wheelchairs and pushchairs, and there is a lift between floors.

Exercise 1.7

1 How many awards has Eureka! won?
2 How many visitors did Eureka! welcome in its first three years?
3 How many interactive exhibits does Eureka! have?
4 What do Eureka! floor staff do?
5 Name two of the four main exhibition areas.

Visiting friends or relatives

Many people spend their leisure time visiting friends or relatives. They may then decide to do some sightseeing with them and visit tourist attractions in the area.

Going to a sports event

We have already looked at how people spend their leisure time by participating in sport or being a spectator. This may involve travelling away from home a short distance or a long distance. Quite often football supporters will travel to Europe, Wembley or other countries to watch their favourite team. People who participate in a particular sport may have to travel to take part.

Travel

Destination
where someone is
travelling to

Tourism will usually involve travel. Travel is about how people get to their chosen **destination**. Some journeys involve travelling long distances whereas other journeys might be more local. Visitors to an area will use a variety of transport such as:

- ✪ **Air**
- ✪ **Rail**
- ✪ **Ferry**
- ✪ **Bus**
- ✪ **Taxi**
- ✪ **Car hire**
- ✪ **Coach**

Air

Travelling by air has become more popular in recent times because it can be quicker than the alternatives and because air fares have become much more affordable.

Many visitors from outside the UK will arrive by aeroplane. There are several airports in the UK, making it easier for people to visit different parts of the country. Here are some of them:

London Heathrow	London Gatwick
Birmingham	Manchester
Leeds/Bradford	Newcastle
East Midlands	Luton
Stansted	Glasgow
Belfast	

A few people may travel by helicopter, but this does not happen very often.

Activity 1.26

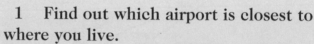

1 Find out which airport is closest to where you live.
2 Name three different **airlines** that use the airport.

▼▼▼▼▼▼▼▼▼▼

Airlines
companies that provide air travel for customers (e.g. British Airways)

▲▲▲▲▲▲▲▲▲▲

Rail

Travelling by train is more common when visiting places within the UK and there are often special rates for families wanting to visit different areas and attractions.

Activity 1.27

You want to meet a friend in London to visit some attractions. You need to arrive in London between 1400 and 1500 hours on Wednesday and hope to be back home by 2000 hours on Friday. Find out:

★ The time of the train you would need to catch from home

★ The cost of a return ticket

The Channel Tunnel has also opened up a rail link to Europe as an alternative to ferries and aeroplanes.

Ferry

Ferries are a popular way of travelling, especially for European visitors who want to come into the UK. There are several ferry companies that offer this service, including:

✪ **Brittany Ferries**

✪ **P&O**

✪ **DFDS**

Some UK-based visitors may want to visit places such as Ireland, the Channel Islands and the Scottish Isles. There are ferries available to take them there.

In addition, some small ferries take customers over lakes and rivers in the UK. For more information, the ABTAC atlas has a very good map of the UK showing the different ferry routes and companies.

Activity 1.28

Find out the name of another two ferry companies and the countries they provide transport to and from.

Road

Buses, taxes, hire cars, coaches – all can be classed as road transport. If you are making a long journey, stay on motorways for as long as possible in order to reduce the travel time.

Most purpose-built major attractions in the UK are close to the motorway network. Figure 1.18 shows a map of the major population centres and motorways in the UK.

Activity 1.29

Using the map on page 59, write down which motorways you would use if you were travelling from your home to either London or Plymouth.

Bus

All towns and cities have a local bus service for travelling around the area. Quite often special services are provided for tourists (e.g. the park and ride scheme in York where tourists can park their car away from the city and then catch a bus into the centre). National bus companies provide links between major towns and cities in the UK (e.g. National Express).

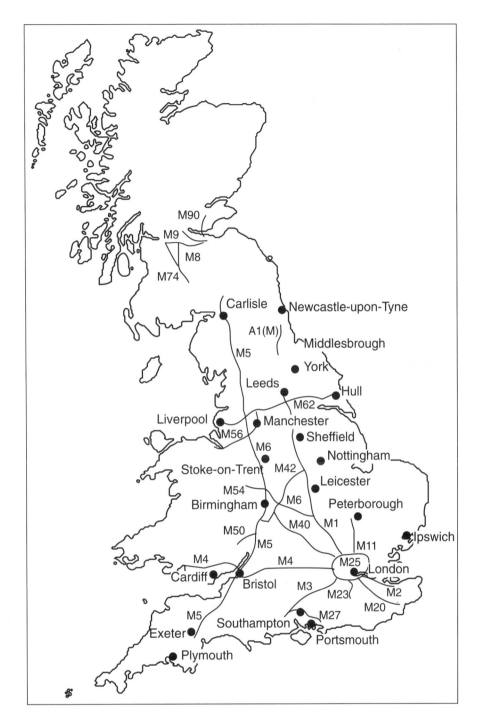

Figure 1.18 *Major population centres and motorways*

Travelling by bus is often cheaper than other forms of transport, but it usually takes much longer and you have to travel at set times.

Taxi

Taxis provide a quick, convenient way of travelling. They can be ordered at any time; they will collect you from wherever you are and take you directly to your destination.

Taxis can be quite expensive and most people only use them for short journeys. If you are travelling with friends, you may be able to share the cost and then a taxi may be cheaper.

Car hire

Tourists may hire a car for many different reasons; here are two:

✪ **They may have flown from a different country and they have left their car behind**

✪ **They may not own a car and want to hire one as a convenient way of travelling**

Cars can be hired for a long period of time or just a day. The cost usually depends on the size of the car and the length of time it is hired for. Three **car hire companies** are Hertz, Avis and Budget.

▼▼▼▼▼▼▼▼▼▼

Car hire companies
companies that allow people to hire a car for a period of time; they usually charge a daily rate

▲▲▲▲▲▲▲▲▲▲

Activity 1.30

Imagine that your sister and her partner have travelled from Geneva in Switzerland to visit you. They have asked you to arrange car hire for them for seven days.

1 Use Yellow Pages to find out how many different car hire companies operate in your local area.

2 Find out the cost of hiring a suitable car for seven days.

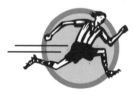

Coach

Travelling by coach is one of the cheapest ways of getting to your destination. Many coach companies will provide transport to popular tourist attractions, including:

✪ **Out-of-town shopping centres:** the Trafford Centre near Manchester, Meadowhall near Sheffield, etc.

✪ **Cities:** London, Bath, York, etc.

✪ **Holiday resorts:** Brighton, Blackpool, Bournemouth, etc.

Travel and tourism in your chosen area

It's now time to look at one particular area in the UK. Choose somewhere that interests you, perhaps a city, a holiday resort or a national park. The rest of the activities in this unit will now concentrate on your chosen area.

You will need to look at the travel and tourism industry in your chosen area and be able to identify what tourism facilities exist for use by residents and tourists such as:

✪ **Tourist information centres**

✪ **Travel agents**

✪ **Visitor attractions**

✪ **Hotels, guest houses and other accommodation**

✪ **Methods of transport (e.g. bus, ferry, train)**

✪ **Tour and guiding services**

▼▼▼▼▼▼▼▼▼
Guest houses
small hotels, usually family-run
Accommodation
somewhere to stay overnight
▲▲▲▲▲▲▲▲▲

Tourist information centres

Areas that attract a large number of visitors each year usually have at least one tourist information centre (TIC). Some TICs are open all through the year, others are open only during the summer or on certain days.

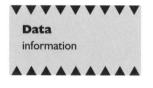

Data
information

TICs have a large amount of information on local services and attractions, including hotels, museums and walks; they also have other interesting **data**. If you know you are going to be visiting an area, the staff can often book your accommodation for you or send useful information to your home address.

Activity
1.31

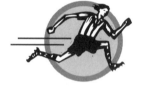

1 Find out if there is a TIC in your chosen area; there may be more than one.
2 Write down the address and telephone number of each TIC in your chosen area.

Travel agents

Travel agents are companies that link people with tour operators, either people travelling abroad or within the UK.

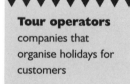

Tour operators
companies that organise holidays for customers

In order to do this, the **tour operators** must make sure the travel agents have all the necessary information on computer and in brochures.

The travel agent can then use this information to give advice and help to customers and make bookings for them with the tour operators. Lunn Poly, a travel agent, may book a family holiday with Thomson, a tour operator.

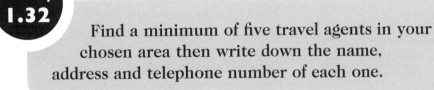

Activity 1.32

Find a minimum of five travel agents in your chosen area then write down the name, address and telephone number of each one.

Visitor attractions

We have already looked at the different types of visitor attraction, but you may want to go back and read about them again. Remember, there are three main types:

- ✪ **Recreational attractions:** national parks, tourist resorts, etc.

- ✪ **Culture and entertainment:** heritage sites, galleries, theatres, etc.

- ✪ **Children's attractions:** theme parks, zoos, children's museums, farms, leisure pools, etc.

Activity 1.33

You have been asked to produce a display for your chosen area that will be mounted in the local library. The display needs to focus on the main visitor attractions in the area and must include a map of the area giving the approximate location of each attraction.

Hotels and guest houses

Most tourist areas offer a wide variety of accommodation, ranging from five-star hotels to youth hostels and campsites.

Accommodation brochures often use a range of standard signs and symbols as a guide to the different types of accommodation; Figure 1.19 shows some examples.

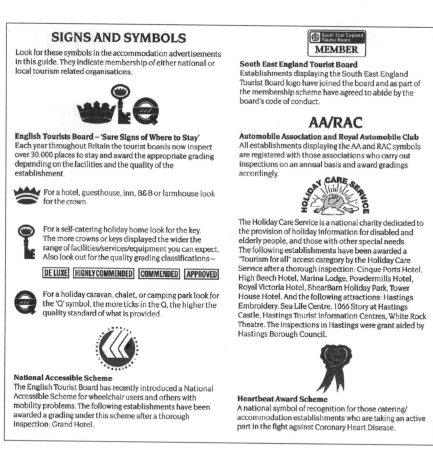

Figure 1.19 *Accommodation brochures use these symbols*

Other standard signs are used for the different kinds of facilities; these are shown in Figure 1.20.

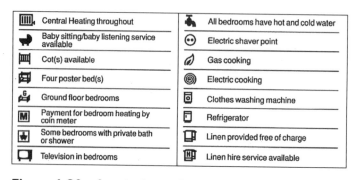

Figure 1.20 *Standard signs for accommodation facilities*

Exercise 1.8

Find out the symbol used for the following facilities and draw it next to the description:

- Babysitting or baby listening service
- Four-poster beds
- Cots available

▼ ▼ ▼ ▼ ▼ ▼ ▼ ▼ ▼

Luxurious
a high standard of accommodation with lots of extras (e.g. a whirlpool bath)

▲ ▲ ▲ ▲ ▲ ▲ ▲ ▲ ▲

Some types of accommodation are expensive and **luxurious**, other types are cheaper and more basic.

Many people prefer to do their own cooking because it is cheaper, and it gives them more freedom and flexibility. It is often much cheaper than staying in hotels and guest houses and it means they can choose what, when and where they eat. Camping, caravanning and staying in flats, apartments or houses are all examples of self-catering accommodation.

Other people may prefer to have someone else doing their catering for them because it means they can have a rest and spend more of their time enjoying themselves. This is called serviced accommodation and people can choose from:

✪ **Bed and breakfast**

✪ **Half board (this includes breakfast and evening meal)**

✪ **Full board (this includes breakfast, lunch and evening meal)**

The standard of serviced or self-catering accommodation can vary enormously; it depends on the price you wish to pay.

Some campsites have heated swimming pools, hot showers, restaurants and entertainment and will be much more expensive than campsites with only a cold water tap. Figure 1.21 shows a self-catering holiday centre.

No.69   12A

COMBE HAVEN
HOLIDAY CENTRE

Harley Shute Road, St.Leonards-on-Sea, Hastings, East Sussex
Telephone (01424) 427891

Ten minutes from Hastings Station, this all action family holiday park has something for everyone.
The facilities include an excellent children's Funpalace and Tiger Club, multi-sports court and hall, large food court and shopping precinct, restaurant and Sussex Inn Pub.
Also live free evening entertainment. For a free colour brochure please call (01914) 174141.

Prices are based on a Haven 7 caravan.

	min £	max £
Per Week	156.00	434.00

Figure 1.21 *Combe Haven is a self-catering holiday centre*
Courtesy Hastings and St Leonards Tourist Board

▼▼▼▼▼▼▼▼▼

Room service
a charged-for service that provides guests with certain things (e.g. food and drink delivery, dry cleaning and ironing)

Gourmet food
food of a high standard

▲▲▲▲▲▲▲▲▲

Some hotels have their own health clubs, swimming pools, private bathrooms, satellite or cable television and offer **room service** and **gourmet food**, whereas small guest houses offer basic food and may expect you to share a bathroom with other guests. Figure 1.22 shows the Queen's Hotel in Leeds, part of the Forte Grand hotel chain.

Activity 1.34

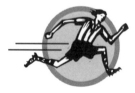

Select two different types of accommodation in your chosen area and list the facilities and services they offer to their guests. If you can, try to find out the costs of staying in each one for three nights (accommodation only).

Figure 1.22 *The Queen's Hotel is part of a chain*
Photo courtesy of Kay Spragg

Methods of transport

Getting about is extremely important to tourists. They will want to know the different types of transport available to them, and quite often they will not want to waste too much of their precious holiday time travelling around.

Most areas will have some of the following types of transport available for visitors:

✪ **Buses**

✪ **Trains**

✪ **Trams**

✪ **Taxis**

✪ **Hire cars**

✪ **Bicycles**

✪ **Coaches**

Private limousines
expensive cars that can be hired by visitors and usually include a driver

Some areas may offer more expensive forms of travel, including **private limousines** with a chauffeur. Here are some other examples:

✪ **Aeroplanes**

✪ **Helicopters**

✪ **Boats, ferries and barges**

Activity 1.35

Find out about the different types of transport available to visitors in your chosen area; make a list of them.

Tour and guiding services

Many places will provide a range of tours and guiding services for people to discover the area and its attractions. Here are some examples:

Guide
a person who shows customers around
Qualified
when someone has passed a test or examination that means that they are able to do something

✪ **Open-topped city tour bus in London:** takes people on a set route around the city; a **guide** will talk about the places of interest on the route

✪ **Tour guide in York cathedral:** a person who takes tourists around the cathedral and gives them information on its history and architecture

✪ **Guided walks by countryside wardens in Calderdale:** these are walks in the countryside led by **qualified** people

✪ **Tours around Cadbury World in the West Midlands:** visitors get taken around the factory and shown the different processes for making confectionery

Activity 1.36

Contact the tourist information centre (TIC) and list at least five different tour and guiding services in your chosen area. Provide a brief description of each one, including costs.

Information sources

There are many different ways to find out about an area's leisure and tourism facilities. Here are some of them:

- ✪ **Yellow Pages**
- ✪ **Local library**
- ✪ **Tourist information centre**
- ✪ **Internet**
- ✪ **Local newspapers**
- ✪ **Other local publications**
- ✪ **Friends and family**

The Internet

Most leisure and tourism facilities now use the Internet to communicate with customers. In many cases you can use the Internet to buy a whole range of goods and services, for example:

- ✪ **Flights**
- ✪ **Holidays**

- ✪ **Videos**

- ✪ **Computer games**

Activity 1.37

Can you think of two more leisure and tourism goods or services you can buy using the Internet?

Here are some leisure and tourism websites you may find useful:

www.jamba.co.uk	Games
www.number.10.go.uk	Tour of 10 Downing Street
www.rac.co.uk	Route planners and traffic news
www.scoot.co.uk	Cinema guide with local listings
www.filmsite.org/	Film reviews
www.scansea.com	Scandinavian Seaways
www.ytb.org.uk/	Yorkshire Tourist Board
www.warnerholidays.co.uk	Warner Holidays
www.ordsvy.gov.uk/educate.html	Ordnance Survey
www.nationalexpress.co.uk	National Express
www.cosmos-holidays.co.uk	Cosmos Holidays
www.ticketweb.co.uk	Tickets for plays and concerts
www.amazon.co.uk	Books, music, videos and games

www.travel.roughguides.com	Travel books and guides
www.easyjet.com	Easyjet information and booking
www.jakarta.co.uk	Games and entertainment
www.thetrainline.com	Rail travel
www.ebookers.com	Travel agent
www.iwm.org.uk/educ/htm	Imperial War Museum, London
www.everwonder.com/david/juggle/	All about juggling
www.funfair.ndirect.co.uk/intro.html	All about funfairs
www.hindleap.co.uk	Outdoor Education Centre
www.earthcentre.org.uk	Earth Centre Ecology Park
www.ballet.org.uk	Information on ballet
www.nmsi.ac.uk/nrm/	National Railway Museum
www.english-heritage.org.uk	English Heritage
www.warwick-castle.co.uk	Warwick Castle
www.hmsbelfast.org.uk	Warship
www.allhealth.com	Fitness experts and advice
www.york-tourism.co.uk	Information on York
www.sportsaid.org.uk	Sport for those with special needs
www.alton-towers.co.uk	Alton Towers

www.visitbritain.com   British Tourism Authority

www.culture.gov.uk   Heritage sites

Activity 1.38

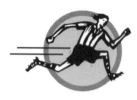

Using all the information sources in this section at least once, find out about the following things in your chosen area:

★ The name and address of a guest house that offers bed and breakfast for under £20.00

★ The name and address of a local video rental shop

★ The cost of hiring a small car for one day and the name of the company

★ Guided walks on offer over the next four weeks

★ The name and telephone number of a local restaurant with disabled access

★ Two films on offer for children at a cinema

★ The name of the performance on offer at a theatre

★ The cost of hiring a badminton court for one hour

★ The opening times of the swimming pool at the weekend

★ The time and day of the next match at a football club

Remember to state where you found the information (which information source you used) and write up all your findings using appropriate computer software.

Promotion in leisure and tourism

2

Facilities
buildings, areas or places offering the goods or services

Customers
people who buy goods and services

All leisure and tourism **facilities** need to let their **customers** know what they have to offer. To do this they use methods known as 'promotional techniques'. These include many things (e.g. leaflets and advertising in newspapers).

In this unit, you will learn about:

- ● **The importance of promotion** ✓

- ● **Promotional techniques** ✓

- ● **Promotional materials used in leisure and tourism** ✓

- ● **The effectiveness of promotional materials** ✓

As well as producing a record of the promotional techniques and materials used by leisure and tourism facilities, you will also design promotional material of your own.

The importance of promotion

THE IMPORTANCE OF PROMOTION

▼▼▼▼▼▼▼▼▼

Advertise
a way of letting people know about your products

Promote
letting people know about the facility, including goods and services on offer

▲▲▲▲▲▲▲▲▲

If a facility (organisation) does not **advertise** and **promote** itself, it probably won't be successful. Customers need to be told various things, such as where the facility is, what it offers, when it is open and how much it charges.

Promotion is part of marketing and covers four main areas, known as the four P's:

✪ **Product:** what goods and services an organisation offers

✪ **Price:** how much the goods and services cost

✪ **Promotion:** how organisations get people to buy their goods and services

✪ **Place:** where the goods and services are offered

Product

▼▼▼▼▼▼▼▼▼

Organisation
business or facility

▲▲▲▲▲▲▲▲▲

In marketing, the term 'product' is used to describe what an **organisation** sells. This can be either goods or services.

Services are a mixture of skills, entertainment and information. When you visit a safari park you are:

✪ **Entertained by being able to watch the animals**

✪ **Guided through the park by trained staff who have special skills**

✪ **Given lots of information as you travel around the park**

None of these things are physical goods and you cannot take them away with you.

As well as providing a service, most leisure and tourism organisations also sell a range of goods, for example:

- ✪ **A safari park may sell postcards, souvenirs and food**

- ✪ **A swimming pool will probably sell goggles, armbands and snacks**

- ✪ **A museum may sell small gifts, postcards and books**

▼▼▼▼▼▼▼▼▼
Profits
the amount of money
left after all the bills
have been paid
▲▲▲▲▲▲▲▲▲

Selling goods helps an organisation to increase its **profits**. Many customers are also very happy when they can take something away to remind them of their visit and when they can buy food and drink while they are there. Figure 2.1 shows a picture of the cafe at Eureka!.

Figure 2.1 *The Eureka! cafe has a menu for children*

Exercise 2.1

1 Match the facilities on the left to the products (goods or services) on the right. We have done the first one for you.

Private beach	Ordnance Survey maps
Children's play area	Holiday brochures
Horseriding centre	Inflatable rings
Art gallery	Life jackets
Water park	Indoor riding lessons
Sailing centre	Prints
Travel agent	High-energy snacks
Youth hostel	Programmes
Multi-gym	Remote-controlled cars
Theatre	Parasols and deckchairs

continued

continued

2 Complete the following table giving two examples of the specific goods and services for each of the different facilities and types of product.

Facility	Type of product (goods or services)	Example 1	Example 2
Theme park	Goods on sale		
Winter holiday resort	Coaching or lessons available		
Outward bound centre	Outdoor activities available		
Theatre	Ways of making bookings		
Swimming pool	Food and drink on sale		

Price

When deciding how much to charge customers for products, organisations have to think about four main things:

✪ **How much the organisation thinks its customers are willing to pay**

✪ **How much competitors are charging for similar products or services**

✪ **How much profit the organisation wants to make**

✪ **What it costs the organisation to provide its products or services**

How much the organisation thinks its customers are willing to pay

There is no point charging a price that no one is prepared to pay, because you will end up with no customers and soon go out of business. What you charge depends on what you are providing and whether other people offer it too. If you are the only organisation providing something, you can often charge more.

Another thing that can affect the price is timing. Here are some examples:

- ✪ **Cinemas sometimes charge less on a Monday evening** because fewer people want to go out to see a film. By doing this they hope to sell more seats on a quiet evening

- ✪ **Gyms often charge much less for daytime membership**; this is to try and get people to use the facilities during the day rather than in the evenings when it is very busy being used by customers who have been working

- ✪ **The cost of hiring a car can vary through the year**; during school holidays cars are often much more expensive to hire

- ✪ **Accommodation in British holiday resorts** is often

cheaper during the winter months (low season) and more expensive during the summer months (high season)

✪ **Hotels in large cities often have cheaper rates at weekends** because most of their customers are business people who stay in hotels mainly during the week

How much competitors are charging for similar products or services

When deciding how much to charge your customers, it is important to find out what other people are charging their customers in order to be competitive. Getting the price right is very difficult; you could charge too much or too little.

▼▼▼▼▼▼▼▼▼

Competitors
other businesses that
provide similar goods
and services

▲▲▲▲▲▲▲▲▲

If you charge too much, you may lose customers to your **competitors**. If you charge too little, you may get a lot of customers but you may not make enough money to pay your bills.

Activity 2.1

1   Choose a video that you would like to hire.
2   Find out the cost of hiring it from six different places.
3   Write down:

a. the cheapest price
b. the most expensive price
c. the average price
d. the difference between the highest and lowest prices

How much profit the organisation wants to make

Profits
the amount of money left after all the bills have been paid

Most organisations want to make a **profit**. When deciding on a price, organisations have to think about the size of their profits.

If the organisation is the only one providing something in the area, it can charge more and make more profit.

However, many leisure and tourism organisations provide similar things, so customers do have a lot of choice. Therefore, in order to keep their customers, organisations sometimes have to charge less than they would like.

What it costs the organisation to provide its products or services

All organisations have bills (costs) to pay. If they cannot pay them, they will go out of business; because of this, they have to make sure they charge enough for their products to cover their costs before making a profit. Here are some typical costs:

- ✪ **Wages**

- ✪ **Heating**

- ✪ **Equipment**

- ✪ **Rent**

Can you think of four more?

Jasbir and Sally have just completed their Vocational A-level in Leisure and Recreation and have decided to open a play gym for under 5s.

They have done a lot of research and have decided there is a need in their town for a leisure facility to serve this age group. They have used £5,000 of their savings and taken out a bank loan of £20,000 to set up the gym.

The cost of running the play gym for one week is:

	£
Rent	100.00
Wages	400.00
Heating, lighting and telephone	70.00
Bank loan	150.00

The gym is open for 6 hours every day including Sundays – a total of 42 hours every week. Jasbir and Sally are going to charge each child £4.00 for a one-hour session in the play gym.

1   Calculate how many children would need to use the play gym each week to:
    a. cover the cost of running the gym
    b. make £100 profit
    c. make £500 profit

2   For each of your answers, work out how many children, on average, will be using the play gym each hour of the week.

▼▼▼▼▼▼▼▼▼
Communicating
letting people know things
Products
good and services
▲▲▲▲▲▲▲▲▲

Promotion

Promotion is about **communicating** with your customers to let them know about your organisation and its **products**. It covers a wide range of activities that are called promotional techniques. We will be looking at this in more depth later in the unit.

Place

Place is very important in marketing. If it is difficult to reach a leisure or tourism facility, customers may not want to make the effort to get there. Equally, many people want to book holidays and buy tickets early rather than just turn up and hope for the best.

▼▼▼▼▼▼▼▼▼

Physical location
the place where the facility is

Agents
people who sell tickets on behalf of a leisure and tourism organisation

▲▲▲▲▲▲▲▲▲

Place mainly covers the **physical location** of the organisation (where it is) or the point of sale (where and how you can purchase tickets and make bookings). For example, tickets for theatre shows are often sold all over the country by **agents** or sent by post to customers who have booked seats by telephoning or writing to the theatre or contacting them via the Internet.

Activity 2.3

1   Obtain a copy of a national Sunday newspaper.
2   Choose two shows that are currently available in London.
3   Write down all the different ways you could book tickets to see them.

Leisure and tourism facilities tend to be located in these areas:

▼▼▼▼▼▼▼▼▼

Population
the number of people
who live in an area

▲▲▲▲▲▲▲▲▲

✪ **Where there is a large population within easy reach**

✪ **Close to major transport routes**

A good example of a leisure and tourism facility built near a large population centre is the American Adventure theme park in the East Midlands. Here are some major population centres, the distance to this theme park and the estimated travel time.

Population centre	Distance (km)	Travel time (minutes)
Birmingham	76	60
Bradford	126	75
Coventry	83	60
Derby	13	20
Leeds	111	60
Manchester	88	120
Sheffield	51	45

Activity 2.4

1   With the help of your teacher, choose a major leisure or tourism facility that is close to a number of large towns and cities.
2   On a map, identify the attraction and the position of the main towns and cities nearby.
3   Choose three of the towns and cities.
4   Work out the distance (km) from the towns and cities to the attraction.

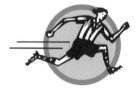

Most leisure and tourism facilities will need to be located close to motorways, railway stations and bus routes to ensure that customers can get to them easily. Figure 2.2 shows a map of the major population centres and motorways in the UK.

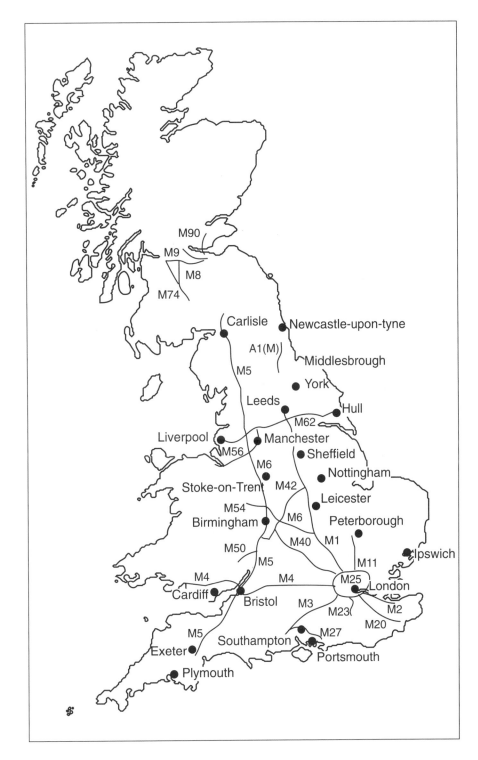

Figure 2.2 *Major population centres and motorways*

1   Using the map on page 85, identify the location of these six major leisure and tourism attractions:

a. Alton Towers

b. Blackpool (tourist resort)

c. Dartmoor National Park

d. York Minster

e. Sizewell Visitor Centre

f. Caernarfon Castle

2 Choose two of the visitor attractions from the above list and, for each one, describe:

a. Which large towns and cities are nearby

b. The motorways that are near to the attraction

Promotional techniques

▼▼▼▼▼▼▼▼▼

Methods
ways of doing
something
Persuade
trying to get someone
to do something

▲▲▲▲▲▲▲▲▲

Promotion is one of the four P's of marketing. Promotional techniques are the **methods** used by organisations to let people know about their products and services and **persuade** them to buy or use them.

Here are some promotional techniques:

✪ **Advertising**

✪ **Direct marketing**

✪ **Public relations**

- ✪ **Personal selling**
- ✪ **Displays**
- ✪ **Sponsorship**
- ✪ **Demonstrations**
- ✪ **Sales promotions**

Advertising

Organisations regularly pay to place advertisements to let their customers know about the products they offer. The most common ways of advertising are newspapers, magazines, television, radio, cinema and the Internet.

However, the costs of advertisements vary. A three-minute advertising slot on television will cost many thousands of pounds whereas a small advertisement in a local newspaper will cost less than £50.

Each organisation has to decide the best method of advertising at a cost they can afford.

Activity 2.6

You work for Ace Leisure Promotions. The Adelphi Theatre (located in a city in the East Midlands) has received some money from the National Lottery Fund and has used it to redecorate the theatre and improve the lighting, sound system and backstage facilities.

They are going to have a grand reopening in a month's time and have asked Ace Leisure Promotions to produce advertising for the new-look theatre.

continued

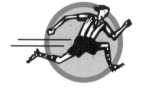

continued

1   In small groups, choose one of the following:

   a. Produce a 60 second video advertisement to be shown on television.

   b. Produce a 30 second radio advertisement.

   c. Produce an advertisement for a local paper.

2   Give your advertisement to another group and ask them to comment on it and suggest any improvements you could make.

Direct marketing

Direct marketing involves sending information and promotional material about the organisation straight to individual customers. It is one of the most popular and fastest-growing promotional techniques used today.

Direct marketing involves two main areas:

✪ **Sending information directly to existing customers:** if you stay in a hotel, you may receive details of special offers a few months later

✪ **Trying to reach potential customers:** it is possible to buy lists of names and addresses of customers from various **companies** who you can then mail with information. A theatre in a major city might want to attract new customers and buy a **mailing list** for sending out their brochure

▼▼▼▼▼▼▼▼▼

Companies
profit-making
organisations
Mailing list
list of names and
addresses that can be
bought

▲▲▲▲▲▲▲▲▲

The cost of direct marketing can vary from fairly cheap to quite expensive. It would not cost very much to put leaflets through the doors of customers living close to your facility. Buying a special mailing list to send out brochures and information to a large number of potential customers would be much more expensive.

Leaflets are often used for direct marketing. The costs involved in producing a leaflet can be broken down into preparation costs and printing costs.

Preparation costs

Before a leaflet is actually produced, a lot of time, skill and money will be used to

✪ **Decide on the content of the leaflet**

✪ **Decide on the size and layout of the leaflet**

✪ **Decide on the quality of the leaflet**

  • **black and white photocopy on one side of A4**

  • **full colour, folded on glossy paper**

✪ **Produce a selection of drafts from which to choose the final version**

- ✪ **Take any photographs that need to be included**

- ✪ **Hold meetings to make final decisions**

Printing costs

Once all the decisions have been made and the draft leaflet produced, the next stage is to print the leaflets. Printing costs come under four headings:

- ✪ **Print run**

- ✪ **Size**

- ✪ **Layout**

- ✪ **Complexity**

Print run

The print run is the number of copies printed. Professional printers often charge different amounts depending on the number of copies required. The more copies you want, the cheaper the price per copy.

Activity 2.7

When using a photocopier, the printing costs will be a certain amount per copy. Imagine each photocopy of a leaflet costs 4p. Calculate how much would it cost to produce:

- ★ 20 copies
- ★ 125 copies
- ★ 2,568 copies

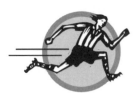

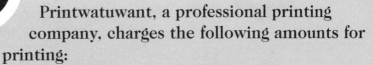

Activity 2.8

Printwatuwant, a professional printing company, charges the following amounts for printing:

1–50 copies	10p per copy
51–1,000 copies	8p per copy
1,001–3,000 copies	6p per copy

Work out how much it would cost for Printwatuwant to print the leaflets from Activity 2.7.

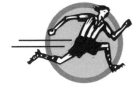

Size

The size of the leaflet affects the cost of printing. It is cheaper to produce A4 size leaflets than larger A3 size leaflets.

Layout

The layout of the leaflet affects the cost of printing. A simple layout (e.g. one sheet of A4 with information on one side) will cost less than a more complicated layout (e.g. one sheet of A4 that is double-sided and folded into three) because it is easier to produce and takes less time.

Complexity of content

Complexity simply means having lots of different things in the leaflet (e.g. drawings, photographs, maps) and using different colours. If the leaflet is very complex it will cost more to produce.

Activity 2.9

1   In a small group find out about the printing facilities in your local area and produce a list; you could look in a telephone directory.

2   Ask your teacher for a leaflet that has been used by a leisure or tourism facility as part of a direct marketing campaign.

3   Find out how much it would cost to produce 500 copies of the leaflet at one of the printers.

4   Compare your findings with those of other groups.

Public relations

▼▼▼▼▼▼▼▼▼▼

Media
methods of communicating to people (e.g. television, radio, newspapers)
Articles
pieces of writing about something

▲▲▲▲▲▲▲▲▲▲

Organisations like to have a positive image. Public relations is known as PR and does not cost the organisation anything at all.

It involves getting the **media** to write **articles** or mention the organisation as part of a feature or programme that is running. Here are two examples:

✪ **A new gym has just opened in a small town:** it has an open evening to attract new customers and invites a reporter who works for the local newspaper. The newspaper decides to write an article, free of charge, about the evening

✪ **A television programme looks at tourism in Bournemouth:** it mentions two hotels and a holiday park and it describes the facilities and charges

▼▼▼▼▼▼▼▼▼▼

Critical
when things are said about a product or facility that are not positive

▲▲▲▲▲▲▲▲▲▲

Remember that publicity can be bad as well as good. Sometimes the reports may be poor or **critical**.

Activity 2.10

You are a reporter for a health magazine. You have been invited for a free weekend to a new health farm on the outskirts of your town. You have agreed to write an article about the health farm to be printed in your magazine.

1   With the others in your group, brainstorm as many different services as you can think of that are usually offered by health farms.

2   Choose one of these services and write a short article for your magazine. The article can be positive or negative – it's up to you.

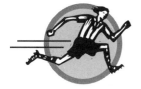

Personal selling

Personal selling always involves a salesperson talking to customers either face-to-face or over the telephone. The salesperson will try to find out about the customer by asking questions. Then they will begin to describe the product and sell it to them.

Personal selling involves contacting existing customers and potential customers; it could be quite expensive because:

✪ **Someone has to be employed and paid for contacting the customers**

✪ **In telephone selling, the telephone calls have to be paid for**

✪ **With home visits, the travel costs of the salesperson have to be covered**

You work for a large organisation that has a number of holiday parks throughout Britain. Your job is to ring potential customers to try and sell them a family holiday at one of the parks. You are going to pair up with another person then role-play some situations.

1   Choose who is going to be the potential customer and who is going to be the salesperson.

2   Together, think of:

   a. Information you need to give to the customer

   b. Questions you will ask to get information about the customer

   c. Answers the customer will give (including personal details)

3   Practise role-playing the conversation and make changes if you need to.

4   Each pair should now perform their role play in front of the other pairs.

5   Who is the best salesperson? Give your reasons.

Displays

▼▼▼▼▼▼▼▼▼

Demonstration
showing people
something
Premises
buildings used by a
business

▲▲▲▲▲▲▲▲▲

A display can often be used by an organisation as part of another promotional activity such as a **demonstration** or sales presentation. However, a display can also be used on its own. Many organisations have a display stand they can put up in their own **premises** or leave somewhere else. Displays can be a relatively cheap sales technique. Here are some examples of using displays:

✪ **A local theatre** has a display in the local tourist information centre; there are photographs, posters, leaflets and brochures for customers to look at or take away

✪ **A video rental shop** has a regular display in the shop showing videos due to be released and any special discounts for customers

Activity 2.12

Produce a display to go up in your school or college. It should promote an activity or facility in leisure and tourism.

Sponsorship

Sponsorship is where one organisation, the sponsor, gives money and support to another organisation or to an event. The sponsor does this because its name will be displayed on the product or at the event. Here are some examples of sponsorship:

✪ **A swimming pool may decide to sponsor a Scouts' swimming gala:** they will let them use the pool free of charge and provide drinks for the swimmers. In return, the

Spectators
people who watch something (e.g. a football spectator will watch a football match being played)
Hotel chain
hotels owned by the same company (e.g. the Queen's Hotel in Leeds is part of the Forte Grand hotel chain)

Scouts will name the pool as their sponsor in all their promotional material and the gala may attract potential new customers as **spectators**

✪ **A large hotel chain may decide to sponsor an ice hockey team:** they provide money to buy all their equipment. In return, the club have the name of the **hotel chain** on the front of their hockey shirts and above their electronic scoreboard. Every time the team play, the name of the hotel is on display

The cost of sponsorship will vary tremendously depending on what you have agreed to give the organisation you are sponsoring.

Here is a photograph of three players from Halifax Roller Hockey Club showing the name of their sponsor, Anglo Canadian Alloys, on their shirts.

Figure 2.3 *Anglo Canadian Alloys sponsors roller hockey*
Courtesy Anglo Canadian Alloys and Halifax Roller Hockey Club

Activity 2.13

Think of five different football clubs then find out who sponsors them.

Demonstrations

Demonstrations are usually given by new organisations that want to attract customers or existing organisations that have new products on offer. They may have open days or open evenings so that customers can see products being used, try them out for themselves and ask questions about them. Quite often the organisation will provide drinks and snacks during the demonstration.

Here are some examples of demonstrations used by leisure and tourism organisations:

✪ **A gym** has bought some new exercise equipment that no other organisation provides locally. They have decided to have three open days to demonstrate the equipment. They invite their existing customers and ask them to bring along two friends

✪ **A new museum** has just opened that is designed for children up to the age of 12. It decides to invite all local teachers from primary schools to a demonstration day to look at the exhibits and the things they can provide for schools' parties

The cost of demonstrations can vary depending on what the organisation decides to do and may depend on:

✪ **How many people are invited**

✪ **How many staff are needed**

✪ **What free gifts are given to customers**

✪ **The type of refreshments provided**

✪ **Whether you need to hire premises to do the demonstration**

Sales promotions

Temporary
for a short period of time
Discount voucher
a type of ticket that allows you money off something

Sales promotions are **temporary** activities that involve giving the customer something to get them interested in the product. These could include:

- ❂ **A discount voucher which can be used by the customer**

- ❂ **Two for the price of one**

- ❂ **A free gift (e.g. a meal or an entrance ticket)**

- ❂ **Entry to a competition**

The sales promotion will probably involve special displays and/or demonstrations to attract customers' attention. The cost of a sales promotion depends on the activity. Usually, the aim is to attract more customers to make more profit and cover the cost of the promotion.

Activity 2.14

For each of the four sales promotional methods listed, try to find an example of how it has been used. For example, Granada Studios in Manchester occasionally offers 'two for the price of one' entrance fees.

When deciding which promotional techniques to use, an organisation will have to think carefully about the following:

How big is the organisation?

Vary
not always the same

Leisure and tourism organisations **vary** in size. Small organisations include guest houses, local theatres and private tennis clubs. Large organisations include hotel chains, theme parks, national museums and national chains of fitness clubs.

Budget available for the promotion

▼ ▼ ▼ ▼ ▼ ▼ ▼ ▼ ▼

Profits
the amount of money
left after all the bills
have been paid

▲ ▲ ▲ ▲ ▲ ▲ ▲ ▲ ▲

The money that an organisation has to spend on promotion will depend on its size and the amount of **profit** it makes. A small guest house may spend less than £500 a year on promotion whereas a large hotel chain will spend many thousands of pounds.

Purpose of the promotion

Before an organisation spends money on promotion it must think about what it wants to promote and why. For example, a small guest house may want to attract some customers in April because it was very quiet that month last year.

Timescale of the promotion

▼ ▼ ▼ ▼ ▼ ▼ ▼ ▼ ▼

Promote
letting people know
about the facility,
including goods and
services on offer

▲ ▲ ▲ ▲ ▲ ▲ ▲ ▲ ▲

Deciding when to **promote** an organisation is very important. Some events will have to be promoted well in advance to give customers enough warning and opportunity to get tickets (e.g. a pop concert). Other organisations may want to promote all year long and will have an ongoing promotional campaign (e.g. a local leisure centre).

Target audience

It is important that all organisations decide which type of customers they want to attract before choosing the promotional techniques to use. They need to make sure their promotional campaign will reach their customers and attract their attention. Here are two examples:

- ✪ **A tour operator** offers expensive cruises. Its target audience will be people who can afford this type of holiday

- ✪ **A local nightclub** has decided to open its doors to under 18s on a Monday night when it is usually closed. Its target audience will be people aged between 14 and 18

Type of product

Appropriate
the most suitable

The type of product being promoted will affect the promotional technique. For example, it would not be **appropriate** to use television advertising to promote a local swimming gala.

Exercise 2.2

Match the **most appropriate** type of promotional technique on the left to the leisure and tourism organisation on the right. We have completed one of them for you.

TV advertisement	Rugby club
Direct marketing	Tour operator (e.g. Thomson)
Public relations	Takeaway restaurant
Personal selling	Tourist information centre
Demonstration day	Theatre
Displays	Video rental shop
Sponsorship	Health club
Sales promotion	Children's museum

Promotional materials used in leisure and tourism

We have covered the eight main promotional techniques used by leisure and tourism organisations.

Exercise 2.3

We have given you the first three letters for each main promotional technique; complete the words.

Adv........

Dir... ....

Pub... ....

Per..... ....

Dis.....

Spo........

Dem..........

Sal.. ....

Most of these techniques will use promotional materials in some way. The main promotional materials are:

- ✪ **Advertisements**

- ✪ **Brochures and leaflets**

- ✪ **Posters**

- ✪ **Point-of-sale items**

- ✪ **Merchandising materials**

- ✪ **Videos**

- ✪ **Press releases**

- ✪ **Computers and the Internet**

Advertisements

▼▼▼▼▼▼▼▼▼

Audio-visual
something that you
can see and hear (e.g.
a video)
Oral
spoken

▲▲▲▲▲▲▲▲▲

Advertisements may be written (e.g. an advertisement in a newspaper, magazine or on a hoarding), **audio-visual** (e.g. an advertisement on the television or at a cinema) or **oral** (e.g. an advertisement on the radio).

Below is an advertisement for Romney, Hythe & Dymchurch Railway taken from a brochure advertising facilities in Hastings and St Leonards.

Figure 2.4 *This steam railway advertised in a Hastings brochure*
Courtesy Hastings and St Leonards Tourist Board

Newspaper advertisements

▼▼▼▼▼▼▼▼

Local
close to where a person lives
Regional
relating to an area of the country (e.g. Merseyside)
National
throughout the whole country

▲▲▲▲▲▲▲▲

Newspapers may be **local**, **regional** or **national**; they may be daily or weekly. Some are free but most have to be paid for.

Advertisements in national newspapers will be read by people all over the country, whereas local or regional newspapers will have a smaller number of readers within a particular area.

Activity 2.15

Have a look at the newspaper circulation figures below then answer the questions that follow:

National newspaper circulation	Jan 2000	Dec 1999	% change	Aug 99-Jan 00	Aug 98-Jan 99	% change
Dailies						
Sun	3,557,336	3,395,273	4.77	3,584,020	3,682,395	-2.67
Mirror	2,270,543	2,178,398	4.23	2,297,405	2,322,550	-1.08
Daily Record	626,646	626,482	0.03	636,947	678,817	-6.17
Daily Star	593,826	596,412	-0.43	609,700	643,516	-5.25
Daily Mail	2,427,888	2,310,781	5.07	2,376,705	2,350,048	1.13
The Express	1,050,846	1,012,573	3.78	1,053,962	1,115,356	-5.50
London Evening Standard	440,287	404,968	8.72	441,228	451,701	-2.32
Daily Telegraph	1,040,931	1,022,937	1.76	1,036,348	1,050,319	-1.33
Times	726,349	709,556	2.37	724,680	751,076	-3.51
Financial Times	435,378	440,381	-1.14	421,893	372,952	13.12
Guardian	401,560	386,767	3.82	394,162	393,231	0.24
Independent	222,106	222,350	-0.11	224,554	221,186	1.52
The Scotsman	75,402	72,079	4.61	75,883	80,362	-5.57
Sundays						
News of the World	4,139,793	3,861,193	7.22	4,093,079	4,244,546	-3.57
Sunday Mirror	2,008,961	1,867,820	7.56	1,989,940	2,000,558	-0.53
Sunday People	1,613,113	1,543,674	4.50	1,583,535	1,718,310	-7.84
Sunday Mail	751,084	746,106	0.67	759,388	n/a	n/a
Mail on Sunday	2,323,720	2,251,905	3.19	2,304,851	2,324,613	-0.85
Sunday Express	974,310	967,815	0.67	977,504	1,024,208	-4.56
Sunday Times	1,373,900	1,298,566	5.80	1,348,604	1,364,403	-1.16
Sunday Telegraph	815,093	820,353	-0.64	822,032	826,194	-0.5
Observer	416,460	406,151	2.54	407,770	402,097	1.41
Independent on Sunday	248,630	245,503	1.27	249,548	254,281	-1.86
Scotland on Sunday	106,514	101,045	5.41	109,114	127,465	-14.40
Sunday Business	70,369	64,356	9.34	61,416	n/a	n/a
Sport First	85,223	86,246	-1.19	93,016	n/a	n/a

Figure 2.5 *Circulation figures for national newspapers*

Courtesy Audit Bureau of Circulations

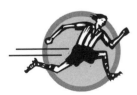

1 Which daily newspaper sold the most copies between August 1998 and January 1999?

2 Which daily newspaper increased its sales by 5.07 per cent between December 1999 and January 2000?

3 How many copies did the *Sunday Mirror* sell between August 1999 and January 2000?

1   Get a copy of your local newspaper.

2   Cut out three advertisements for local visitor attractions.

3   Using £5.00 per square centimetre, work out how much each of your chosen advertisements would have cost.

To advertise in a newspaper, you have to pay a certain amount of money depending on:

✪ **The size of the advertisement**

✪ **The number of times the advertisement is to appear**

✪ **The type of newspaper**

- **national**

- **local**

- **regional**

Magazine advertisements

Advertisements in magazines tend to be more colourful and glossy than those placed in newspapers and will therefore be more expensive.

Published
produced and
available for sale

Magazines may be **published** weekly, fortnightly, monthly or even every few months; they can be divided into two types:

✪ **General magazines:** *Woman's Own, Family Circle, Hello* etc.

✪ **Specialist magazines:** these focus on hobbies and interests, e.g. *Caravan Life*

Hoardings

Hoardings are like large framed posters and are often placed along busy roads where a lot of people can see them. Because they are so big, they catch people's attention very easily. Usually they just have a very simple message, with pictures and colour, because people tend to see them for a short time as they are passing.

New electronic hoardings are appearing in large towns and cities. They allow more than one product to be promoted by changing the image on a screen every few minutes.

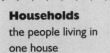

Activity 2.17

On your way home from school or college, list two hoardings that you spot and what they are advertising.

Television advertisements

Households
the people living in one house

The most expensive and the most effective kind of advertisement is a television advertisement; this is because 97 per cent of **households** in the UK have at least one television set.

Although expensive, large leisure and tourism organisations will often use television advertisements because they reach so many people. There are 13 commercial television stations that show both national and regional advertisements. Costs vary depending on the television channel (e.g. Channel 5), the time and the day.

Exercise 2.4

Find the 13 television stations hidden in the following wordsearch.

Meridian/Channel	Anglia	Westcountry
Ulster	Border	Carlton/LWT
Central	Granada	Yorkshire
Tyne Tees	STV	Grampian
HTV		

```
M E R I D I A N C H A N N E L
A B E C D E N F A D A N A R G
G H T I J K G L R M N O P E Q
R S S T U V L W L X Y Z A D B
C D L E F G I H T I J K L R M
N G U O T P A Q O R S T U O V
W R X Y Z Y A B N C B E F B G
H A I J E K N L L A R T N E C
N M N O R P Q E W R S T U V W
X P Y Z I A B C T D E F G H I
J I K L H M N O P E Q H R V S
T A W V S W X Y Z A E B T C D
E N F G K H I J K L M S N V O
P A Q B R C R D G H L M J K A
V W X A O B C Z X D E F Z Y G
X H I M Y R T N U O C T S E W
```

Cinema advertisements

Advertisements used in cinemas have the same advantage as television advertisements because they use sound, colour and movement. But they are less expensive as they do not reach as many people.

Radio advertisements

▼▼▼▼▼▼▼▼▼

Commercial
concerned with
commerce and
making a profit
Rates
charges

▲▲▲▲▲▲▲▲▲

There are at least 140 **commercial** radio stations. There are national stations (e.g. Virgin Radio) but most of them are local and therefore ideal for advertising local leisure and tourism organisations.

The cost of a radio advertisement is far cheaper than the cost of a television advertisement. **Rates** vary depending on the radio station, the time of day and the day of the week.

Activity 2.18

1   Find out which local radio stations are listened to by people in your group.

2   Produce a bar chart or a pie chart to display this information, whichever you think is more suitable, using appropriate computer software.

3   Identify any advertisements for local leisure and tourism organisations that your group have heard on the radio recently.

Brochures and leaflets

Brochures and leaflets are the most common promotional materials used by leisure and tourism organisations. Their size and shape depend on the amount of information to be included. Many are printed on A4 paper that is folded into three.

Tourist information offices, hotels, guest houses and libraries often keep stocks of leaflets and brochures for the major attractions in their area. Figure 2.6 shows the inside of a leaflet for Eyam Hall.

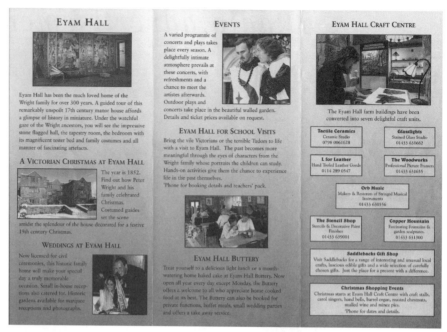

Figure 2.6 *Eyam Hall's leaflet is an A4 sheet folded into three*
Copyright Eyam Hall 2000

Activity 2.19

1 Collect five different leaflets and brochures advertising local visitor attractions.

2 Look at each one and summarise the information under the following headings:

★ Location

★ Times

★ Prices

★ Facilities

★ Special events or attractions

★ Services

★ Pictures or drawings

3 State which one you like the best and why it appeals to you.

Posters

Posters usually give similar information to leaflets and brochures but they are much larger. All the details are printed on one side so the poster can be displayed on walls and windows.

Notices are similar to posters, but rather than generally advertising a leisure or tourism facility, they usually include:

✪ **Maps**

✪ **Transport timetables**

✪ **Opening times**

✪ **Special events**

Activity 2.20

Simba's Circus is coming to town. Design a poster, to be displayed locally, giving the following information:

★ Circus begins 10 May and finishes 24 May
★ Located in the Everglades Park
★ Three performances every day at 1400, 1700 and 1930 hours
★ Three ticket prices:

Adults	£6.50
Children up to 14, senior citizens and unemployed	£4.00
Family discount ticket (2 adults and 2 children)	£19.00

★ Ring 01323 671234 to make advance bookings

Here are some examples of point-of-sale items in leisure and tourism facilities:

Souvenirs
things that people buy to remind them of their visit

✪ **Sweets and snacks at a cinema**

✪ **Goggles and armbands at a swimming pool**

✪ **Guidebooks at a museum**

✪ **Postcards and souvenirs at a zoo**

Activity 2.21

1 Think of two more leisure and tourism facilities you have visited and list the point-of-sale items that are usually available for customers to buy.

2 Can you think of any other items that customers would like to have available at these facilities?

Merchandising

Merchandising is about promoting goods and services at the point of sale. Merchandising materials include anything that can be used to display products or promotional information.

Figure 2.7 shows the shop at Eureka! in Halifax and the inside of the shop at Eyam Hall in Derbyshire.

Activity 2.22

1 In small groups, visit a local travel agent.

2 List the merchandising materials at the travel agent and what they were used to promote.

3 Design and make a window display in your base room to promote holidays in London.

Figure 2.7 *Souvenir shops at Eureka (left) and Eyam Hall*

Videos

Many large leisure and tourism organisations, such as theme parks, hotels and holiday resorts, now provide customers with videos so they can actually see what is on offer in the comfort of their own home.

Activity 2.23

1 Find a video promoting a leisure or tourism organisation; your teacher should be able to provide you with one.

2 Watch the video and answer the following questions:

a. How long did the video last?

b. Did it use well-known personalities (e.g. an actor or sportsperson)?

c. What information did it give you (e.g. prices, opening times)?

d. What age group did it seem to target?

e. Did it keep you interested?

f. Did it make you want to visit the attraction?

g. How do you think it could be improved?

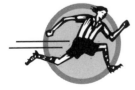

Press releases

Sometimes leisure and tourism organisations may want to let customers know about special events or new products and services. As well as using advertising, leaflets, brochures and posters, they may also want to use press releases.

A press release is given to journalists and usually contains a story about the organisation, its products or services. The journalists may work for newspapers, magazines, radio or television; and the press release may include photographs, ready-written articles or a story idea for the journalist. Below is a press release from the Royal Armouries in Leeds.

Figure 2.8 *A press release from the Royal Armouries in Leeds*
Courtesy Royal Armouries

Activity 2.24

1   Imagine you are the publicity officer employed by a large castle.

2   A national television company wants to produce a programme in the grounds of the castle. The programme will ask people to bring along their unusual pets (e.g. singing dogs and exotic lizards).

3   Put together a press release for the event to give to local newspapers and television companies, using appropriate software.

Computers and Internet

Computers and the Internet are becoming one of the most popular ways of promoting leisure and tourism organisations.

When a leisure or tourism facility designs promotional material, it should try to include all the information customers may need.

Activity 2.25

Here are some websites used by different leisure and tourism organisations:

★   www.warwick-castle.co.uk
★   www.earthcentre.org.uk
★   www.nmsi.ac.uk/nrm/

1   Look at the information on these webpages or go to the websites of other facilities which interest you more. Look at the kinds of information they give to their customers.

2   Design a website for a leisure and tourism organisation of your choice.

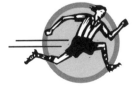

Effectiveness of promotional material

Some promotional materials will attract more customers than others. This is usually because of the way they have been designed, the words they use, their availability to customers and the images they use.

It is quite easy to make promotioinal materials more attractive to customers. Here is a list of things that can make them more effective:

▼▼▼▼▼▼▼▼▼
Slogans
short phrases and
words that are used
to attract people's
attention
▲▲▲▲▲▲▲▲▲

- ✪ **Bright colours**

- ✪ **Eye-catching graphics**

- ✪ **Slogans**

- ✪ **Bold headlines**

- ✪ **Photographs of personalities or celebrities**

- ✪ **Clear and simple messages**

- ✪ **Explanations of the benefits to the customer**

Bright colours

Colour is an easy way of making materials more attractive. But remember that the more colour you use, the more you will have to pay. Different colours attract different age groups. A children's museum would probably choose very bright colours such as red, yellow, blue and green.

Activity 2.26

1   Collect a range of different leaflets used to promote visitor attractions.
2   Do a survey to find out which colours the different age groups find attractive.
3   Produce a chart showing the results of your survey.

Eye-catching graphics

Graphics include things like drawings, charts or pictures. Most computers have graphics software that can be used to make text more interesting. When using graphics, they should be relevant to the text and placed where they will attract the customer's attention.

Activity 2.27

Using the leaflets you collected for Activity 2.26, choose the two that you feel have the most eye-catching graphics. Give your reasons.

Slogans

Slogans are short phrases and words that are used to describe a facility. They are designed to be easily remembered and attract customers.

The Royal Armouries in Leeds run educational programmes for teachers and pupils. Their brochure has this slogan: Education that fires the imagination.

Here are some other slogans used by organisations:

- **Number one for summer camp fun! (Camp Beaumont)**

- **Unwrapping the package holiday piece by piece (JMC Tour Operator)**

- **Where great family holidays are made! (Haven Holidays)**

Activity 2.28

1   Think of six different slogans that you remember; they do not have to be about leisure and tourism.
2   Write a slogan for a theme park of your choice.

Bold headlines

Bold headlines are used to stress important messages. These are often used by newspapers and magazines. Size, font and style are used to make headlines stand out and attract attention.

Activity 2.29

1   Using the slogan you have written for a theme park, produce 10 different ways of displaying it for use on an A4 leaflet.
2   Which one do you prefer? Why?

Celebrity photographs

Photographs of celebrities are often used to attract customers' attention then perhaps they will read the promotional material. Remember that different celebrities will attract different age groups.

Activity 2.30

Complete the following table by entering three well-known personalities or celebrities that would attract the different age groups.

Age group	Personality 1	Personality 2	Personality 3
Children under 12			
Teenagers			
Adults			
Senior citizens			

Clear and simple messages

The information given on promotional material must be short, to the point and contain all the relevant details. If it is too long, customers will not read it.

Explanations of the benefits to the customer

Highlights
makes something stand out and get noticed

Make sure any promotional material **highlights** the benefits to customers of visiting or using the facility. Include a statement like this: something for all the family. But choose words that fit your product.

Activity 2.31

1 Collect five brochures and leaflets for leisure and tourism facilities.

2 For each example:

a. Write down the types of customer the explanation would attract.

b. List the benefits to the customers.

Activity 2.32

1 Look at the promotional material for the Royal Armouries in Leeds (Figure 2.9). Now answer these questions:

a. Are there any eye-catching graphics or bold headlines?

b. Do they use any slogans?

c. Is the writing clear and simple?

2 In pairs, discuss the material and what they are trying to tell their customers about the Royal Armouries.

3 Imagine that you have been asked to suggest the name of a well-known personality or celebrity that could be used to promote the Royal Armouries. Who would you choose and why?

4 List the name of a sponsor of the Royal Armouries in Leeds.

THE EDUCATION CENTRE

The Education Centre provides a wide range of services, catering for all ages from nursery to adult. Teacher's packs and a large number of worksheets and lesson styles offer support not just for those interested in history but also for students of art and design, technology and science – even maths! First-hand learning using both original and replica artefacts offers a stimulating and unique experience for all of our students. For further information telephone 0113 220 1888.

Education supported by

THE LIBRARY

The Royal Armouries library is a world-class facility comprising nearly 40,000 books, pamphlets and journals. Most of these relate directly to the Museum's collections, the history of arms and armour and the history of the Tower of London. The collection includes manuscripts and early books. The picture library mainly covers collection objects: there are about 150,000 black-and-white photographs and about 2,000 colour transparencies. The main library is housed in Leeds, and is open free of charge between 10.30 am and 4.30 pm, Monday to Friday (not including Bank Holidays). For further information please telephone 0113 220 1832.

For more information about the Royal Armouries visit our website at www.armouries.org.uk

Figure 2.9 *Promotional material for the Royal Armouries*
Courtesy Royal Armouries

To successfully complete this unit, you will need to produce a piece of promotional material of your own design that a leisure or tourism organisation could use. Here is an activity to help you practise.

You are employed in the marketing department at a theme park in your area. The marketing director has decided to organise a large campaign to promote the theme park and attract extra visitors. The theme park is going to offer a free second day in the park to everyone who visits in the next two months.

She has decided that it would be a good time to do this as a pop concert is going to be held at the park in two months' time to raise money for charity and the campaign can cover both the 'free second day' offer and the pop concert.

The marketing director has asked you and your colleagues to design leaflets that could be used as part of the campaign. She will then compare the leaflets to decide which one to use.

On your own, design a leaflet that includes the following information:

★ A map or directions on how to get to the theme park

★ Details of public transport available to get to the theme park

★ Information about the special 'free second day' offer

★ What there is to see and do at the attraction

★ What age groups will enjoy visiting the attraction

★ Opening times

★ Prices

★ Details about the pop concert

★ Information about the facilities available for customers with special needs

★ Terms and conditions about the special 'free second day' offer

continued

continued

★ Reservation telephone numbers

You must also make sure that the leaflet has:

★ Bright colours
★ Eye-catching graphics
★ A slogan
★ Bold headlines
★ Photographs of well-known personalities or celebrities
★ Clear and simple messages
★ Explanations of the benefits to the customer.

Decide on the information to put into your leaflet (e.g. opening times and prices). You may find it helpful to use leaflets produced by similar theme parks.

Ask your teacher to comment on your leaflet and suggest any improvements you could make.

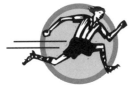

Exploring customer service in leisure and tourism

3

In this unit you will find out about:

- **The importance of customer service**

- **Personal presentation**

- **Types of customer**

- **Dealing with customers**

- **Contact with customers**

- **Reasons for customer service**

The importance of customer service

All leisure and tourism facilities need to make sure their customers are happy with the service they receive, because customers are the most important part of any successful business.

Giving a very good level of customer service can bring the following benefits:

- ✪ **Increased sales**

- ✪ **Satisfied customers**

- ✪ **More customers through repeat business and recommendations**

- ✪ **A better public image**

- ✪ **An edge over the competition**

▼▼▼▼▼▼▼▼▼
Satisfied customers
customers that are pleased with goods or services
▲▲▲▲▲▲▲▲▲

Besides creating **satisfied customers**, the staff will be happier and more likely to take a pride in their work if they feel they are providing excellent customer service.

Increased sales

Facility
the building, area or place offering the goods/services
Guidance
advice and help

Most leisure and tourism facilities will want to increase their sales because this will bring more money into the business and help it to be successful. Providing effective customer service could mean that customers will prefer one **facility** to another. For example, a gym that provides one-to-one advice and help to its customers will probably increase its sales and have more customers than a gym that leaves customers to use the equipment without any **guidance**.

Satisfied customers

If a customer is not happy or satisfied with the service they have received, they will probably never return and the facility may go out of business.

It is important to be able to tell if your customers are happy. **Dissatisfied customers** will probably:

Dissatisfied customers
customers that are not pleased with goods or services

- ✪ **Not use your service**

- ✪ **Look unhappy or annoyed**

- ✪ **Make a complaint**

- ✪ **Walk out and never return**

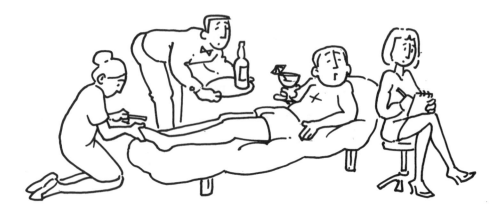

Colleagues
people who you work with
Reputation
what customers think about the facility

Satisfied customers will probably tell their friends, family and **colleagues** about how good the facility is, and this will help to improve its **reputation**.

There are several ways to find out whether your customers feel happy with the service they have received. A satisfied customer will probably:

✪ **Use your service regularly**

✪ **Look interested and ask questions**

✪ **Talk positively about the facility to**

- **friends**
- **family**
- **colleagues**

Repeat business

Lots of leisure and tourism facilities rely on the same customers coming back again and again in order to survive. This is known as repeat business and is very important.

Customers may also tell their friends, family and colleagues and recommend that they also visit the facility. This is known as word of mouth recommendation.

In this way, the facility not only keeps its existing customers, it also attracts new ones without the need for expensive advertisements and marketing.

Activity 3.1

Name three different leisure and tourism facilities that you have visited because you have heard they have a good reputation and treat their customers well.

Better public image

Image is all about how you appear to other people. Later in this unit you will be looking at your personal image and what kind of message you give to others by the way you appear. Image is also important to leisure and tourism facilities and covers areas such as:

- ✪ **Health and safety**

- ✪ **Security**

- ✪ **Cleanliness**

- ✪ **Quality of staff**

- ✪ **Public relations**

Health and safety

Health and safety is one of the most important things that leisure and tourism facilities must consider. Leisure and tourism customers often take part in activities that could involve some risks, for example:

- ✪ **Swimming**

- ✪ **Horseriding**

- ✪ **Step aerobics**

- ✪ **Rock climbing**

Exercise 3.1

Look at the swimming pool cartoon on page 130 and spot the six different health and safety risks.

There are other potential risks that may not be so obvious, for example:

- ✪ **Staying in a hotel:** if there is a fire, it is important that the guests know where the fire exits are

- ✪ **Eating food:** it needs to be cooked properly in a clean **environment** to avoid food poisoning)

Environment
place, room or area

- ✪ **Travelling by coach:** the vehicle should be roadworthy

- ✪ **Visiting historic sites:** there may be dangers from crumbling walls or poor paving

- ✪ **Rides at a theme park:** if the equipment is not checked regularly it could be extremely dangerous

Activity 3.2

Complete the following table, giving three possible dangers to customers for each of the different facilities. We have completed the first one for you.

Facility	Danger 1	Danger 2	Danger 3
Swimming pool	Drowning	Slipping	Dirty water
Large hotel			
Gym			
Museum			
Theme park			
Theatre			

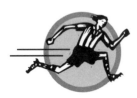

Activity 3.3

You and your friend have just won a million pounds on the national lottery. You have decided to buy a hotel with 12 bedrooms.

In small groups think about what you, as the new owners, will have to provide to make sure that your guests, employees and the hotel itself are as safe as possible.

Write up your list on a flip chart to show the other people in your class and so you can compare your list with those of other groups.

Security

▼ ▼ ▼ ▼ ▼ ▼ ▼ ▼

Facility
the building, area or place offering the goods or services

Possessions
things that people own

Belongings
things like bags, clothing and money

Secure
safe

▲ ▲ ▲ ▲ ▲ ▲ ▲ ▲ ▲

Security in leisure and tourism facilities covers a large number of different things. When people visit a leisure and tourism **facility** they often have to leave their **possessions** somewhere safe. It is important they can trust the staff to look after their **belongings** and not worry that they may get stolen or lost. Customers will also want to feel **secure** and safe from any danger or threat.

Here are some examples of customer security:

✪ **At a bowling alley** people leave their shoes at **reception** where they are safe

✪ **In a hotel** people leave their clothes in their rooms and sometimes put things of value in a hotel safe

✪ **In their car parks** many leisure and tourism facilities now provide security cameras and sometimes even guards

✪ **When flying somewhere** all hand luggage is put through a special X-ray machine to check the contents for dangerous items such as guns and bombs

✪ **Most nightclubs** employ door staff to stop unwanted visitors

✪ **Information leaflets** are sometimes given to **tourists** to help them avoid dangers in foreign countries

▼▼▼▼▼▼▼▼▼
Reception
the area where visitors to the facility are dealt with first of all
▲▲▲▲▲▲▲▲▲

▼▼▼▼▼▼▼▼▼
Tourists
people who are visiting an area in their leisure time
▲▲▲▲▲▲▲▲▲

Figure 3.1 *Airport luggage goes through special X-ray machines*

Activity 3.4

1   In pairs, add three more examples of customer security to those given above.

2   Here is a list of the different ways that leisure and tourism facilities keep their buildings and grounds secure. Choose six of them and complete the table. For each security measure,

continued

Keypads
security device on a door (similar to a telephone keypad) with a special code that has to be punched in to gain entry

Security beams
beams of light that are used to protect something; they will set off an alarm if someone walks through them

Unauthorised entry
entry to an area by someone who has not been given permission to be there

continued

give an example of how it is used in a facility, e.g. secure fencing may be used to protect a theme park like Alton Towers. **Keypads** and **security beams** may be fairly hi-tech.

★ Secure fencing to stop people from getting in
★ Only having one entrance
★ Employing night security guards
★ Fitting burglar alarms
★ Security beams
★ Keypads with special numbers to stop **unauthorised entry**
★ Sniffer dogs
★ Baggage checks

Type of security	Type of facility

Cleanliness

One of the easiest ways of giving a good impression to your customers is to be spotlessly clean. Even poorly decorated facilities can look nice if they are kept tidy and free from litter and dirt.

It is also very important that everyone who works at the facility is clean and tidy; we will look at this later in the unit.

Quality of staff

First impressions are usually the ones that stay with customers forever. If someone is rude to a customer or cannot answer fairly simple questions then they will give a bad impression of the facility.

Skills
things that employees
can do (e.g. use a
keyboard)
Employ
give someone a job
Basic skills
the minimum skills
needed for a job

Different staff will need different **skills** depending on the job they do, and they may need some form of training. It is obviously better to **employ** staff with the necessary skills in the first place, because this is cheaper than having to train them. However, when it comes to effective customer service, all staff will need several **basic skills**.

Exercise 3.2

1   Find the following words in the wordsearch. We have done the first one for you.

Pleasant	Polite	Friendly	Helpful
Patient	Informative	Confident	Willing
Honest	Reliable		

A	B	C	Y	L	D	N	E	I	R	F
D	E	P	O	L	I	T	E	F	G	H
R	H	E	L	P	F	U	L	I	P	J
E	K	O	L	E	M	N	O	P	A	Q
L	R	S	N	T	A	U	V	W	T	G
I	X	Y	Z	E	A	S	B	C	I	N
A	D	E	F	G	S	G	A	I	E	I
B	J	K	L	M	N	T	O	N	N	L
L	C	O	N	F	I	D	E	N	T	L
E	V	I	T	A	M	R	O	F	N	I
P	Z	K	A	J	H	U	W	X	J	W

2   Choose two of the skills you have found in the wordsearch. Write down why you think they are needed by staff who work in leisure and tourism facilities.

3   Choose two skills that describe you and say why.

Public relations

Impression
what a customer thinks about a facility, service, goods or member of staff
Discount
reduction in the amount to be paid

Quite often facilities will help the public in order to create a good **impression**. They may:

✪ **Sponsor local sports teams and provide them with kit**

✪ **Give schools and local organisations a special discount rate for using the facility**

✪ **Help local and national charities by giving them free tickets or a membership they can use to raise money in a raffle**

All these things help to give a positive image to the public about the services being offered.

Competitive edge

Most leisure and tourism facilities have competitors who provide similar services. In order to make a profit and attract customers away from competitors a facility can:

✪ **Charge less for similar services**

✪ **Provide better customer services**

✪ **Run competitions and provide special offers**

✪ **Accept different types of payment**

All these things can help to give an edge over the competition and attract a larger number of customers away from a competitor's facility.

Activity
3.5

Think of two theme parks that you have visited. Which did you prefer and why?

Personal presentation

▼ ▼ ▼ ▼ ▼ ▼ ▼ ▼ ▼

Employees
people who work for
leisure and tourism
facilities

▲ ▲ ▲ ▲ ▲ ▲ ▲ ▲ ▲

The way that you present yourself can give a good image or a poor image of you and your facility. In leisure and tourism, dealing with the public is one of the major tasks of most **employees**, so your image is extremely important.

You must understand the importance of all the following areas:

❂ **Dress**

❂ **Personal hygiene**

❂ **Personality**

❂ **Attitude**

❂ **Behaviour**

Dress

Different facilities will have different rules about the way staff must dress. Many of them will provide a uniform (this could be a T-shirt and cap or a full set of trousers/skirt, shirt/blouse and jacket). Look at the clothes worn by a receptionist at the Queen's Hotel in Leeds.

Figure 3.2 *Look at the clothes worn by this receptionist*

**Activity
3.6**

Describe or draw the sort of clothing you think would be suitable for the following employees:

★ A children's courier at a holiday village
★ An air steward
★ A chef
★ A receptionist in a hotel
★ A guide in a museum
★ A rock climbing instructor

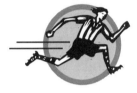

Personal hygiene

Although dressing correctly is important, also make sure you are always clean and tidy. A member of staff who smells, has dirty fingernails, scruffy hair and dirty teeth will give a very bad impression to customers.

Because a lot of work in leisure and tourism facilities is physical work, it is even more important that you wash regularly and use antiperspirant to ensure you do not smell.

Personality

We all have different personalities. They influence how we behave, respond and feel towards other people and situations at work. Your personality will also affect the way that other employees and customers react and respond to you.

It is important that you know and understand your own personality as it will help you to identify things about you that you may need to control. For example, if you lose your temper easily, you may find it difficult to deal with angry customers and this may cause you to lose your job. However, if you are very helpful and caring, you may find that you are given extra responsibility and you could even be promoted.

Exercise 3.3

Here are some words that could describe your personality traits:

Adaptable	Snobby	Confident
Thoughtful	Easy-going	Outgoing
Friendly	Honest	Organised
Aggressive	Ambitious	Caring
Competitive	Arty	Reliable
Emotional	Funny	Lazy
Stubborn	Nervous	Happy
Daring	Hard-working	Shy
Trustworthy	Silly	Helpful

If you do not understand a word, look it up in a dictionary.

1 Choose four words from the list that in your opinion describe you the best – be honest.

2 Ask two friends to choose their four words to describe you.

3 Did you and your friends choose the same four words? Do other people see you the way you see yourself?

4 Look at all the words you and your friends have chosen to describe you then circle those you think would be good personality traits when you start work.

5 Now underline the words that you think would not be very good personality traits when you start work. What do you think you should do about them?

Attitude

Attitude describes how you deal with something. A person's attitude may seem good or bad. At work, we often have to do jobs we do not like (e.g. cleaning equipment). It is important to have a positive, good attitude no matter what job you are asked to do. A negative or bad attitude will upset customers and colleagues.

Behaviour

The way you behave with friends and family will probably be very different to the way you behave with customers and colleagues. Here are some examples of good behaviour in the workplace:

- **Being punctual**

- **Being polite**

- **Being pleasant**

- **Being friendly**

- **Being patient**

There are many more; can you think of any?

Think about situations when you were a customer and someone behaved badly towards you. Give five examples and in each case say how you felt at the time.

Types of customer

Without customers, leisure and tourism facilities would not exist. It is important to remember there are different types of customer, all with different needs. Here are some of them:

- ✪ **Individuals**

- ✪ **Groups**

- ✪ **People of different ages**

- ✪ **People from different cultures**

- ✪ **Non-English speakers**

- ✪ **People with specific needs**

  - • **wheelchair access**

  - • **childcare**

- ✪ **Business men and women**

▼▼▼▼▼▼▼▼▼
Tastes
things that people like
(e.g. someone's taste
in music might be
heavy rock)
▲▲▲▲▲▲▲▲▲

Individuals

Customers are all individuals with different needs and **tastes**; it is important to make sure the services on offer are suitable for them.

Activity 3.8

A new **leisure complex** is going to be opened in your town. They want to know the types of service they should offer to meet the needs of local people. With help from your teacher, design a questionnaire and do a survey of each individual in your group to find out what they want and need.

▼▼▼▼▼▼▼▼▼

Leisure complex
a large facility offering a range of leisure and/or tourism services

▲▲▲▲▲▲▲▲▲

Groups

When providing customer service for groups, remember that the people in each group are still individuals.

People of different ages

Below are some guests at the Queen's Hotel in Leeds. How many different age groups can you see?

Figure 3.3 *How many different age groups can you see?*

Customers can be divided into different age groups. Each of these groups may need certain types of customer service. Some holiday companies provide activities for different age groups (e.g. teen clubs and ballroom dancing competitions).

Exercise 3.4

Complete the table by inserting the following words in the correct places:

Off-season breaks   Activity information pack
High chair   with colouring competition
Disco   Supervised play area
Bar

Age group	Needs
Babies	
Toddlers (1–4)	
Under 12s	
Teenagers (adolescents)	
Adults	
Senior citizens	

People from different cultures

Staff who deal with customers need to know how to look after people from different cultural backgrounds. Differences between cultures include:

✪ **Dress codes:** some Muslim women may keep their legs covered

✪ **Religious needs:** some people need certain times and places to pray

○ **Dietary needs:** some people need special foods, e.g. low-fat milk or halal meat

It is very easy to upset and offend someone without realising it, so staff training may be necessary.

Activity 3.9

Contact a leisure or tourism facility and find out how they deal with customers from different cultural backgrounds.

Non-English speakers

Leisure and tourism facilities often have customers who do not speak any English at all; they need to provide extra services such as:

○ **Leaflets in different languages**

○ **Guides and translators**

  • **German tour at 1400 hours**

  • **Japanese tour at 1500 hours**

○ **Headphones and tapes in different languages**

X*S'''XX* (HAVE YOU GOT THE INFORMATION IN MARTIAN?)

People with specific needs

Customers with visual impairments

▼▼▼▼▼▼▼▼▼

Braille
a way of communicating in writing to blind people by using raised dots that they read by touch

Procedures
set ways of dealing with something

▲▲▲▲▲▲▲▲▲

Some customers will be totally blind and others may not be able to read notices. Many facilities provide special types of service for these customers such as **Braille** signs; others will just make sure the customer understands essential information such as safety **procedures**.

Customers who have mobility problems

Most facilities now provide special equipment such as ramps, lifts and toilets for people who have a problem with walking.

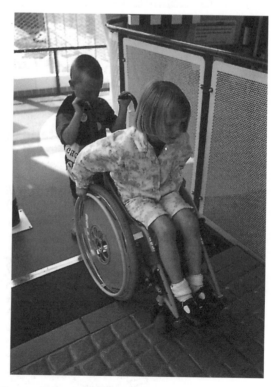

Figure 3.4 *Ramps help children at Eureka!*
Courtesy Eureka! The Museum for Children

Customers with hearing impairments

Quite often customers have a problem with hearing. They may be totally deaf or just unable to hear noises unless they are very loud. Most leisure and tourism facilities now have written notices and information. However, there could be a problem with things like fire alarms.

Customers who have difficulty with literacy or numeracy

If a customer has a problem with reading, signs and information booklets will not be very useful and staff may have to explain certain things **verbally**.

Someone who has a problem with **numeracy** may need help when making payments or using equipment that involves numbers (e.g. exercise machines).

These specific needs are not always obvious and some customers may try to hide them because they are embarrassed. It is important that staff are trained to spot the problems and deal with them **tactfully**.

Verbally
saying rather than writing something
Numeracy
the ability to use numbers to solve problems
Tactfully
doing something without upsetting someone

Customers with young children

Customers with young children can sometimes find it difficult to use facilities. They quite often need somewhere quiet and private to feed and change a baby.

Some facilities now provide special changing and feeding areas and they even offer services such as heating up baby food and bottles.

Customers may also need somewhere secure to store buggies and other equipment.

Business men and women

Leisure and tourism facilities that want to attract business people often have to provide special services for them. This is because they are usually short of time and very busy.

Here are some examples of the services provided to business people:

Environment
place, room or area
Employed
having a job
Conference
a large meeting of business people

✪ **Trains** provide special carriages for people to travel first class. The services on these carriages include free drinks, more space in order to work and a comfortable, quiet **environment**. All these things are very important when you spend a lot of time travelling to meetings and different business organisations

✪ **Gyms** are often open from very early until very late, which allows people who are **employed** to attend them before and after work. They may also offer special company membership schemes for all employees from a certain business

✪ **Large hotels** now provide a wide range of services for business people. Examples are special reduced rates for block bookings, **conference** rooms and equipment, special telephone lines for laptop computers in bedrooms, fax and photocopying facilities and early breakfasts

Figure 3.5 shows some plans of the conference rooms available for business use at the Queen's Hotel in Leeds; they are taken from the hotel's conference brochure. And here is a list of the other facilities the hotel provides for business people:

✪ **Meeting rooms**

✪ **Overhead projectors**

✪ **Flip charts**

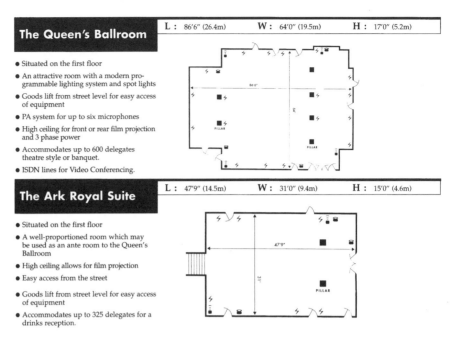

The Queen's Ballroom	L : 86'6" (26.4m)	W : 64'0" (19.5m)	H : 17'0" (5.2m)

- Situated on the first floor
- An attractive room with a modern programmable lighting system and spot lights
- Goods lift from street level for easy access of equipment
- PA system for up to six microphones
- High ceiling for front or rear film projection and 3 phase power
- Accommodates up to 600 delegates theatre style or banquet.
- ISDN lines for Video Conferencing.

The Ark Royal Suite	L : 47'9" (14.5m)	W : 31'0" (9.4m)	H : 15'0" (4.6m)

- Situated on the first floor
- A well-proportioned room which may be used as an ante room to the Queen's Ballroom
- High ceiling allows for film projection
- Easy access from the street
- Goods lift from street level for easy access of equipment
- Accommodates up to 325 delegates for a drinks reception.

Figure 3.5 *Business customers may require conference rooms*
Courtesy the Queen's Hotel, Leeds

✪ **Secretarial services**

✪ **Exhibition areas**

✪ **Videos and monitors**

✪ **Microphones**

✪ **Buffets and banquets**

Figure 3.6 on page 149 shows the types of equipment that the hotel provides. Can you name all the items?

Activity
3.10

1   In groups of three or four individually contact a large hotel in your area to find out the services they offer business people.

2   Share your information with the others in your group and make a list of all the services on offer.

1   On your own, complete the following table. For each of the different types of customer, give two different examples of services that may be provided for them by leisure and tourism facilities. We have done the first one for you.

Customer type	Examples
Individuals	1 Vegetarian meals 2 Single rooms
Groups	1 2
People of different ages	1 2
People from different cultures	1 2
People who speak little English	1 2
People with specific needs	1 2
Business people	1 2

2   a.   Show your table to someone else in your group and tell them why you think facilities should provide the examples you have given.

b.   Get the other person to explain the examples in their table.

3   Do you agree with each other? If not, why not?

Figure 3.6 *Can you name the equipment in this picture?*

Dealing with customers

▼▼▼▼▼▼▼▼▼▼

Policies
guidelines or
documents that tell
you how to deal with
situations

▲▲▲▲▲▲▲▲▲▲

Most leisure and tourism facilities will have **policies** on how to deal with customers and will usually provide training for staff. But there are some basic rules to remember when dealing with customers:

✪ **Always be polite**

✪ **Never argue with a customer**

✪ **Always listen carefully to what customers are saying**

✪ **Do your best to assist customers**

✪ **Be aware of any special needs that customers might have**

✪ **Get help from a supervisor or manager if you cannot handle a situation or if you do not know the answer**

Always be polite and never argue

Always be polite, friendly and helpful to customers, even if they are rude or angry. If staff look bored, ignore customers or are rude to them, this will give a bad impression.

Although you must always be polite to customers, if you are too polite then customers may think you are being sarcastic or that you are trying to avoid a problem by being nice.

Arguing with customers never works and creates a bad impression. It also makes them more angry and less likely to agree with your point of view.

When dealing with customers, you must remember that **non-verbal communication** is just as important as the words you are saying.

Non-verbal communication
a way of letting someone know how you feel without saying anything (e.g. by smiling, frowning, leaning forward)

Activity 3.12

Here are two situations. For each situation write a paragraph on how you would deal with it. When you have written your paragraphs, choose one of the situations and do it as a role play with somebody else.

▶ **IMAGINE YOU ARE A HOTEL RECEPTIONIST**

An angry guest tells a hotel receptionist that the room they have been given is dirty and cold. The receptionist smiles and says, 'Oh dear, that must be dreadful' and continues to smile even though the guest is obviously upset.

continued

continued

▶ **IMAGINE YOU ARE A LIFEGUARD**

A swimming pool lifeguard has to deal with a group of teenagers who are running around the pool, jumping in the water near small children and upsetting other customers. The lifeguard politely asks them to stop doing this but they tell him to get lost and mind his own business. The lifeguard pushes one of the teenagers into the pool and walks off.

Always listen carefully

Sometimes, customers do not say exactly what they want or find it difficult to communicate their wishes clearly. A good listener always:

✪ **Listens with their eyes as well as their ears:** by looking at the person who is speaking, you will also be able to recognise the non-verbal signs and see if they match the words being said

✪ **Asks questions:** if you do not fully understand what someone is saying, you should always ask questions until you are sure you have got the correct information

Do your best to assist

Most facilities will give their staff some form of training to make sure they can deal with customers effectively. They may also provide written standards for customer care, which may include things like:

- ✪ **What to do in an emergency**

- ✪ **How to deal with accidents**

- ✪ **How to deal with complaints**

- ✪ **Who in the facility is responsible for what**

▼▼▼▼▼▼▼▼▼
Expectations
things that customers feel should be provided by facilities
▲▲▲▲▲▲▲▲▲

You will often hear the phrase 'the customer is always right' and this is true most of the time. Most facilities try to meet the needs and **expectations** of their customers. However, there will always be some customers who expect services that the facility does not offer, for example:

- ✪ **Guests at a small hotel may expect room service at 0300 hours**

- ✪ **Customers at a dance studio may expect classes to be provided at every hour of the day**

- ✪ **Some gym members may expect to be able to hire specialist clothing and equipment when the gym does not provide it**

Remember that you cannot always please everyone but it is important that you try to, wherever possible.

Before you can help a customer you need to find out what assistance the customer needs.

Activity 3.13

For each of the following customers, list the type of help and assistance they might need; do not list information and advice, just help and assistance.

★ Crying child in a large museum
★ Man in wheelchair visiting a theatre
★ Woman with hearing aid checking into a hotel
★ Man with guide dog on a day coach trip
★ Woman, on holiday abroad, who has lost her credit cards

Be aware of customers' special needs

We have already covered how different customers have different needs, and some customers may have special needs (e.g. wheelchair users and people with babies). Some of these needs are obvious and others are difficult to spot.

Get appropriate help

If you cannot help your customers because you do not know the answer or you have not been trained in a particular area, you should pass them on to someone who can.

Activity 3.14

Here are some examples of customers with problems:

★ A tourist comes into the tourist information centre and tells the receptionist that her car will not start

★ A swimmer twists his ankle quite badly and is unable to walk. He shouts to you for help

★ An elderly visitor at a castle tells you that she feels unwell and is unable to walk any further

★ Customers at a theatre find other people sitting in their seats who are refusing to move. They ask you to sort it out.

For each of these situations:

1 Decide whether you would deal with the situation yourself or pass the customer on to someone else.

2 If you decide to deal with the situation yourself, describe what you would do. If you decide to pass the customer on to someone else, say who you would refer them to and explain why.

Contact with customers

There are different ways of dealing with customers. Staff in leisure and tourism facilities should be able to provide effective customer service through contact with them.

Face-to-face

Dealing with customers face-to-face is very personal because the customers can see you and you can see them. It can be difficult, especially if the customer is angry, because you then have to deal with the situation immediately and do not have much time to think about what you are going to say and do.

In writing

Some customers prefer to write to a leisure facility rather than speak to someone face-to-face or over the telephone. This is because they can think about what they want to say and keep a copy of their letter as it may be useful later.

Quite often it will be necessary for you to communicate with customers in writing. Figure 3.7 shows a typical letter from a theatre to a customer.

```
                                    VARSITY THEATRE
                                    Chancery Lane
                                    LONDON
                                    L21 4DH

                                        Tel: 01238 55655
                                        Fax: 01238 55555

26 November 20..

Mr Chris Evans
22 Boocock Lane
KIRKDALE
KR21 5GH

Dear Mr Evans

GIRLS GALORE CONCERT - DECEMBER 18

Thank you for your request for six tickets
for the above concert and your cheque for
£72.00.

I enclose the tickets and a seating map
along with details of forthcoming concerts
which you may find interesting.

I hope you have an enjoyable evening.

Yours sincerely

LOIS CRAKER

Encs
```

Figure 3.7 *A typical letter from a theatre to a customer*

Activity 3.15

You work as a trainee assistant in a tourist information centre and have received three letters from customers that need a letter in reply. Your task is to write those letters.

You can make up the information; you do not need to know all the specific details. The address of the tourist information office is 24 Copper Street, York YO15 9TD.

1   Mr Butterworth of 27 Grenwick Square, Cardiff C21 4GH has written asking for a list of hotels in York that cater for guests with dogs.

2   Ms Clare Graham of The Grange, Meadow Lane, Perbury-on-Sea, Essex EX29 3FR has requested details of places of historical interest to visit, including opening times and prices.

3   Mrs Yasmin Iqbal from Kirkdale High School, Crown Street, Kirkdale KR3 2QR wants to know which major leisure and tourism attractions in York give reductions for school parties.

Over the telephone

The main difference between communicating with customers face-to-face and communicating with them by telephone is that you cannot see them when you are talking to them over the telephone and they cannot see you.

Most of the time customers will expect you to deal with them instantly. However, the main advantage with the telephone is that you can ring the customer back if you do not have all the information to hand.

Activity 3.16

1   In pairs, write out a script for the telephone situations below. You will have to make up details such as names and telephone numbers.

2   Take turns at being the customer and act out your scripts.

3   Make any changes to the scripts that you feel are necessary after the role play.

4   List the changes and give reasons for them.

★   A customer telephones a tour operator about an advertisement in the local paper for a coach holiday. The customer wants some information.

★   A guest rings up to see if a hotel has found a wristwatch they lost while staying there two days ago.

When you work in a leisure and tourism facility it is important that you can use all three methods of communicating with customers and understand their advantages and disadvantages.

Activity 3.17

Complete the following table, giving two advantages and two disadvantages for each method of communication

Communication method	Advantages	Disadvantages
Face-to-face	1 2	1 2
Over the telephone	1 2	1 2
In writing	1 2	1 2

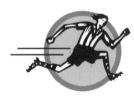

No matter what type of contact you have with customers, the following things are extremely important:

- ✪ **Presenting an appropriate personal image**
- ✪ **Listening to the customer and responding appropriately**
- ✪ **Having good product and service knowledge**
- ✪ **Using appropriate body language**
- ✪ **Asking appropriate questions to find out what the customer wants**

Let us look at each of them in turn.

Presenting an appropriate personal image

▼▼▼▼▼▼▼▼▼
Impression
what a customer thinks about a facility, service or member of staff
▲▲▲▲▲▲▲▲▲▲

When dealing with customers you should always greet them politely: Good morning, how may I help you? This helps to create a good first **impression** and makes customers feel welcome. When writing to customers it is more difficult and you have to be very careful to make sure you cannot be misunderstood.

Listening to the customer and responding appropriately

We have already discussed the importance of listening to the customer carefully and how you might do this. The way you respond is also very important and you need to:

✪ **Be patient while listening**

✪ **Speak slowly and clearly**

✪ **Avoid using jargon that may confuse customers**

▼▼▼▼▼▼▼▼▼
Jargon
phrases that only certain people understand which may confuse customer (GNVQ may not be understood by people outside your course)
▲▲▲▲▲▲▲▲▲▲

✪ **Remember to make notes if you need to take a message**

✪ **Know who to pass customers on to**

✪ **Repeat the customer's main points in order to**

  • **make sure you understand instructions**

  • **be accurate with phone numbers and addresses**

Activity 3.18

1   In groups of three, role-play the situations below. Follow these guidelines:

★ Each person in the group must take a turn at being the member of staff and the customer.

★ Before doing the role play, you may want to carry out some **research** by visiting or telephoning leisure and tourism facilities.

★ You may be able to collect some brochures and leaflets in order to find out **relevant** information

2   Spend some time deciding what you are going to say as part of the role you are playing.

3   After each role play, make a list of the answers, help and assistance given by the member of staff.

4   As a group, discuss the list and add anything else that would have been useful but which wasn't covered during the role play.

▶ **SITUATION 1**

★ *Member of staff:* a courier in a Spanish holiday resort

★ *Customers:* a young couple with two children aged 1 and 4 years who have never been abroad before

▶ **SITUATION 2**

★ *Member of staff:* a riding instructor at a large riding and pony trekking centre

★ *Customers:* two teachers from a special school who want to bring 15 children to the centre. The children have a variety of special needs, including hearing, visual,

continued

▼▼▼▼▼▼▼▼▼
Research
finding something out
Relevant
useful, to the point and necessary
▲▲▲▲▲▲▲▲▲

continued

mobility, behavioural, literacy and numeracy

► **SITUATION 3**

★ *Member of staff*: a trainee tourist information officer working in York

★ *Customers*: two adult foreign visitors who have never been to York before and who speak very little English

Having a good product and service knowledge

When using a leisure or tourism facility, customers will usually want to ask questions about the product or service; it is important that staff can answer most of them. Here are some typical questions:

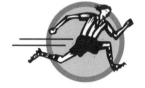

Crèche
area where young children and babies can be looked after while their parents are busy

✪ **What time does the swimming pool open on Tuesdays?**

✪ **How much does it cost to play badminton for an hour?**

✪ **Can I pay my hotel bill by credit card?**

✪ **Do you have a crèche?**

Using appropriate body language

Body language is how people communicate without words; it is also known as non-verbal communication. Non-verbal communication involves:

- ✪ **Eye contact:** look at the person you're talking to

- ✪ **Facial expressions:** use facial expressions to back up what you're saying; you could smile when you greet someone

- ✪ **Gestures:** use your hands to support what you're saying; you could point to something you're describing

- ✪ **Clothing:** wear appropriate clothes for the type of work you're doing; jeans would not be appropriate for a receptionist in a large hotel

- ✪ **Posture:** stand tall and never slouch

Activity 3.19

Look at the pictures and write down what you think the boy is feeling in each case.

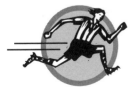

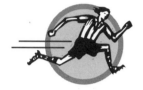

Activity 3.20

Pair up with another person then communicate three different things to them without speaking or using facial expressions (e.g. shrugging your shoulders if you do not know the answer to something). Now let them communicate three things to you.

Activity 3.21

Give three examples of messages sent out by different types of dress or ways of dressing. Maybe think about the way you dress for different activities and what your clothes say about you.

Asking appropriate questions

To help customers, staff should be able to identify the types of information they need. This is usually done by listening to them carefully and asking them questions to find out exactly what they want.

Many facilities have a record card or booking form that customers need to complete; it may ask for personal information such as the customer's age and health.

There are two types of question you need to know about: open questions and closed questions.

Closed questions

Closed questions only allow the person asked to give one answer and are useful if you do not want to spend a lot of time talking about things that are not important. Here are some examples of closed questions:

- ✪ **Would you like an early morning wake-up call?**

- ✪ **Would you prefer to travel by car, minibus, coach or train?**

- ✪ **How old are you?**

- ✪ **Would you like to buy a ticket that lets you visit the gardens as well as the castle?**

- ✪ **Would you like an en suite room?**

Open questions

If a facility offers a large range of services, it might be better to ask an open question instead of listing all the services. Here are some examples of open questions:

- ✪ **What sports are you interested in?**

- ✪ **What did you enjoy most about the film?**

- ✪ **Why are you unhappy with the service?**

- ✪ **Where would you like to visit during your holiday?**

Activity 3.22

You are a trainee hotel receptionist and today you are on duty at the main reception desk of a large city-centre hotel. This means that you will have to deal with lots of people face-to-face and by telephone. For each of the following four situations, and working in a pair:

1   Write down the questions you would ask to identify the information required by the customers.

2   Indicate whether the question you have asked is a closed question (C) or an open question (O).

Here are the four situations:

★   An elderly couple have walked into the reception area of your hotel and want to check into their room. They say they booked a two-week stay with someone, by telephone, three weeks ago.

★   A French businesswoman who speaks very little English has telephoned the hotel to find out if there are any single rooms available and what types of facilities your hotel has.

★   The local tourist information office telephones the hotel to see if it offers any special discounts for families.

★   A young man in a wheelchair comes into reception and would like a room for four nights. He has already tried three different hotels but they do not have the facilities he requires.

Reasons for customer service

One of the main reasons for having effective customer service is to increase sales and have an edge over the competition. However, customer service is not always about selling something to the customer. It also covers:

- **Providing information and advice**
- **Receiving and passing on messages**
- **Keeping records**
- **Providing assistance**
- **Dealing with problems**
- **Dealing with customer comments and complaints**
- **Offering extra services**

Providing information and advice

Making sure that customers have the correct information is one of the main services provided by many different leisure and tourism facilities. For example:

Fire procedures
list of things that must happen if there is a fire (e.g. get out of the building a certain way)

Booking procedures
the system used for booking something (e.g. a seat at a theatre or on a plane)

- **Hotels** usually provide information about meal times, **fire procedures**, local places of interest and their own facilities (e.g. a swimming pool and a hairdresser)

- **Leisure centres** provide information on prices, activities, class times and **booking procedures**

- **Travel agents** provide information on exchange rates for currency, different countries, holidays and locations that are suitable for disabled travellers

Complete the following table giving two examples of information you expect to be available at each facility.

Type of facility	Types of information
National park	1 2
Zoo	1 2
Theme park	1 2
Museum	1 2
Campsite	1 2

Customers can get advice from tourist information centres and visitor centres. However, all leisure and tourism facilities should be able to give their customers honest advice about what they offer.

Even when customers have basic information about a facility, they sometimes require additional advice. Perhaps a family with a very young baby may need advice on which hotel will cater for them best.

1   Imagine you are a Japanese tourist visiting London. List three different types of advice you might need about leisure and tourism facilities.

2   You are a wheelchair user and want to use your local swimming pool. Name two types of advice you may need.

Receiving and passing on messages

Dealing properly with messages is very important. All staff must be able to receive messages correctly and pass them on quickly to the correct person.

Suppose a customer phones up your hotel to cancel their booking and you happen to answer the telephone.

You must ask appropriate questions to find out their name, address, telephone number and date of booking. You must then make sure the receptionist gets all this information in order to cancel the booking in the hotel records.

When taking messages you should:

Vital
important and
necessary

- ✪ **Always write down the essential information**

- ✪ **Listen carefully to what is being said**

- ✪ **Repeat back vital information**

- ✪ **Pass on the message to the correct person**

Activity 3.25

Design a form that could be used by employees for taking messages.

Keeping records

To provide effective customer service, facilities need to keep the following information about their customers:

- ✪ **Complaints**

- ✪ **Enquiries**

- ✪ **Requests**

- ✪ **Sales**

- ✪ **Personal details**

- ✪ **Financial details**

▼▼▼▼▼▼▼▼▼
Discounts
reductions in the
amount to be paid
▲▲▲▲▲▲▲▲▲

Customer information can be used for several different reasons, including letting customers know about future events. A theatre might have a mailing list to let customers know which plays and concerts are coming up in the next few months. Customer records can also be used to let people know about any special offers or **discounts** and any new products or services.

▼▼▼▼▼▼▼▼▼
Accurate
done correctly with
no mistakes
Legible
clear and easy to read
▲▲▲▲▲▲▲▲▲

Filling in customer records is very important and all employees need to be aware of potential problems if it is not done correctly. All records must be **accurate**, **legible** and filed in the correct place.

Look at the completed maintenance card below. It hasn't been filled in very well and it's difficult to read.

1 What is the room number?
2 What is the fault?

Figure 3.8 *Poor handwriting may be hard to read*
Courtesy the Queen's Hotel, Leeds

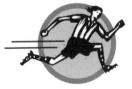

The content of the record must be correct and it must give all the necessary information. If customers want some information sent to them and the record does not detail the type of information, how will you know what to send?

To make sure that all vital information is available, most facilities will use records with:

- ✪ **Set headings** to guide staff on the type of information required, such as name and telephone number

- ✪ **Set amounts of space** under each heading that give an idea of how much to write; if there are four lines to detail a customer's complaint, 'didn't like food' may not say enough

The badly completed maintenance card (page 171) had been left with the receptionist at a hotel. The receptionist simply took the form without looking at it and now has problems because:

- ✪ **She does not know whether the guest is staying in room 410 or 416**

- ✪ **She can make out the word telephone, but nothing else**

Activity 3.27

You work in a large hotel and a guest tells you the sink is blocked in their bathroom.

1   Design a form that can be used to record this information.
2   Complete the form recording the complaint about the sink; make up any details you do not know (name, room number, etc.).

Records of customer complaints

Customers may have several reasons why they are unhappy with the services from a given facility. Make sure all complaints are recorded so that any problem areas are spotted and dealt with as quickly as possible.

Figure 3.9 *Hotels often place cards in the guest rooms*
Courtesy the Queen's Hotel, Leeds

Customers may complain face-to-face, over the telephone or in writing. The facility needs to have a set procedure to deal with the complaint effectively. Here is an example:

- ✪ **A record book** where staff enter details of the complaint and pass on a copy to a senior member of staff

- ✪ **A standard complaints form** that is completed by the customer and dealt with by a senior member of staff within a certain period of time

Below is a blank maintenance card that guests can use if they have a problem with their room. They simply complete the card and give it to the receptionist.

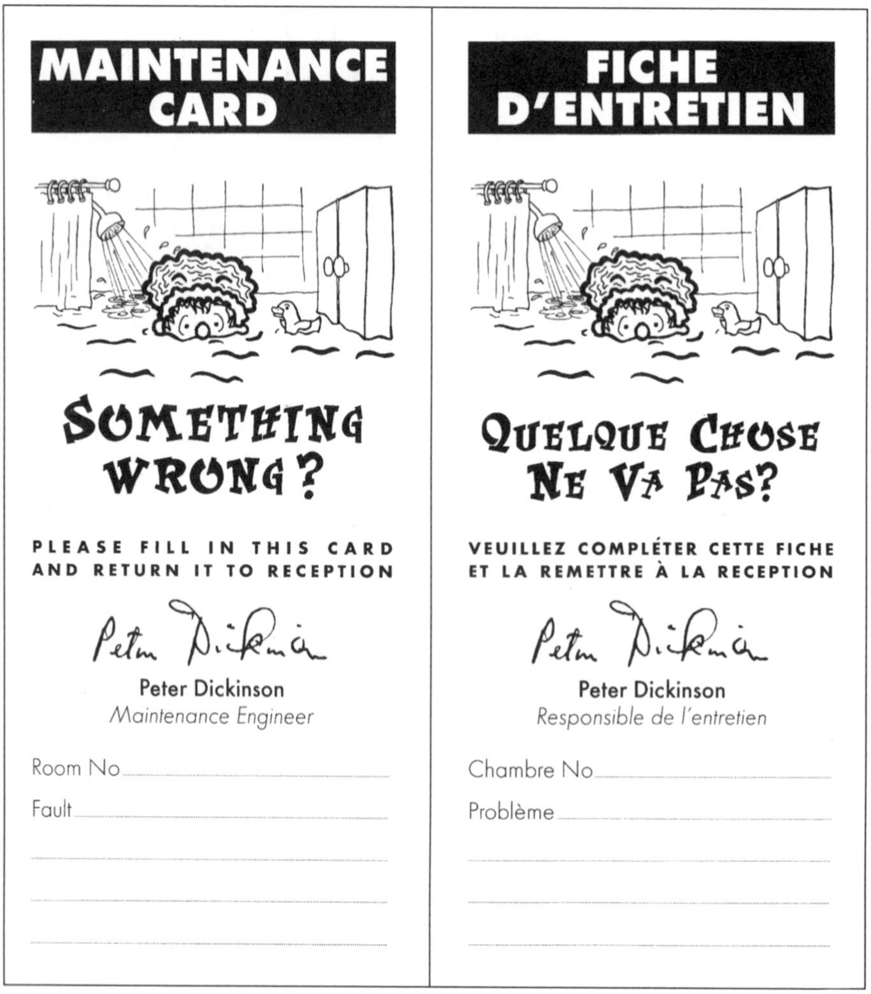

Figure 3.10 *Guests complete a card if they discover a fault*
Courtesy the Queen's Hotel, Leeds

Notice that the card is in two languages (one on each side) to help guests who may not speak or write English very well.

Enquiries and requests

Management
the people responsible for running an organisation

Some facilities may want to keep a record of any enquiries or requests made by customers. This helps them to know what their customers want. If enough customers ask about late opening times at a bowling alley, the **management** may consider staying open for an extra hour, two nights per week.

Sales records

It is very important to keep records of the number of sales. No facility wants to offer services or products that do not sell, because this will cost money and reduce profits.

It also helps to know which services are popular, then the facility can provide more of them to meet the demand.

Customer details

▼▼▼▼▼▼▼▼▼
Health problem
a type of illness (e.g.
epilepsy, diabetes)
▲▲▲▲▲▲▲▲▲

Some leisure and tourism facilities have to keep more detailed customer information than others. For example, a gym may need to know if a customer has a **health problem**. Customer information can be broken down into two main areas: personal details and financial details.

Personal details

Customers using a facility will quite often be asked lots of things about themselves, such as their name, address, date of birth and telephone number. They may also be asked their weight, health record and other things that would be classed as private.

Many facilities have a standard record card with headings or they use a computer database to enter personal information.

▼▼▼▼▼▼▼▼▼
Credit card
thin plastic card that
customers can use to
buy goods and
services (e.g. Visa,
Mastercard)

▲▲▲▲▲▲▲▲▲

Financial details

Sometimes customers will have to give a facility information about their finances such as their **credit card** number or bank account details. It is very important to keep this information secure and you may find that only certain staff have access to it.

```
MEMBERSHIP APPLICATION - SUPERFIT GYM

Name:                              Date of Birth:

Address:                           Telephone Number:




Work Contact Number:

Type of Membership required: (full/step classes only/cardio-vascular only)

Bank details:
Name of Bank:
Address:
Branch Code:
Account Number:


Please sign the agreement overleaf.
```

Figure 3.11 *Membership forms may ask for these details*

Many leisure and tourism facilities have a membership application form that customers complete with their personal details; you can see an example above.

Many customers who want to pay for services over a longer period of time will complete **direct debit** mandates or **standing orders**. These forms have headings that ask for **confidential** banking details and the customer's signature.

A customer joining a gym may want to pay a certain amount of the fee each month by direct debit. They will have to give the gym the name and address of their bank and the number of their bank account. The gym can then arrange monthly transfers from the customer's bank account into the gym's bank account.

▼▼▼▼▼▼▼▼▼
Direct debit
a way of making payments directly from a bank account
Standing orders
ways of making payments directly from a bank account
Confidential
keeping something private
▲▲▲▲▲▲▲▲▲

Think of two more situations when it would
be necessary for a customer to give a leisure
facility personal and financial information.

Information systems

Depending on the size of the facility, the services and products it
has on offer and the number of customers who use it, there are
two ways that customer records can be kept: paper-based
information systems and computer-based information systems.

Paper-based systems

▼▼▼▼▼▼▼▼▼▼

Maintain
keep something up to
date or look after
something

▲▲▲▲▲▲▲▲▲▲

Small facilities, such as riding stables and guest houses, will probably
keep their customer records using a paper-based system because it
is fairly inexpensive, easy to set up and easy to **maintain**. They
may use forms, cards or record books depending on the
information they want to keep.

Computer-based systems

Nowadays even some small facilities keep customer records on
computer, and large facilities (e.g. travel agents, theme parks and
hotel chains) will almost certainly keep their records that way.

A database package is the most common method for keeping
customer information on computer. Here are the main advantages
of using a database:

✪ **It can be quicker**

✪ **It can be more secure**

✪ **It can combine information**

Deleted
crossed out or
removed

Passwords
code words given to
certain people so they
can access
information (e.g. a
word or letters keyed
into a computer to
open a file)

Combine
putting two or more
things together (e.g. a
mailing list combines
customers' names and
their addresses)

✪ **It can save on space**

✪ **Records can be deleted or added**

Passwords can be used to stop certain employees accessing information. Using a database you can search for all customers who live in a certain area; you can search for all customers over age 50; then you can **combine** these two searches to find all customers in a certain area aged over 50.

Whether you use a paper-based or computer-based information system for keeping records, your customers will expect their information to be treated as private and confidential. They will be annoyed if their personal or financial details are given to people without their permission.

There are several different ways that customer records can be kept safe and secure:

✪ **Filing cabinets can be locked and keys only given to certain employees**

✪ **Record cards can be kept behind the reception area where other customers cannot see them**

✪ **Passwords can be installed on computers that stop certain employees from gaining access to information**

**Activity
3.29**

You are the manager of a private golf course. You have paper-based and computer-based systems for keeping customer records. What would you do to maintain the confidentiality of your customer records?

Providing assistance

Some customers will need assistance when using leisure and tourism facilities. For example, a blind person may need help to find a seat when attending a concert.

Exercise 3.5

Match the customers on the left to the types of assistance on the right. We have completed one of them for you.

Customers	Types of assistance
Parent of a baby	Translator
Group of school children	A supervised crèche
A senior citizen	Taking to a quiet area in order to pray
Person who speaks little English	Educational guide
Large family with children of different ages	Help getting a buggy through a turnstile
A vegan	Providing a comfortable seat
A group of Muslim visitors	Help in selecting food from a menu

Dealing with problems

Quite often you will have to deal with a variety of problems when assisting customers. Here are some of them:

- ✪ **Injury**

- ✪ **Theft**

- ✪ **Illness**

- ✪ **Getting lost**

- ✪ **Violence and attacks**

- ✪ **Losing tickets, credit cards or money**

- ✪ **Missing a plane or other transport**

All staff in all facilities should be fully trained to deal with problems themselves or they should know the right person to contact for help.

Dealing with customer comments and complaints

We have already looked at how to spot unhappy customers. Remember that customers can be dissatisfied for a variety of reasons (including poor service) and that different customers react in different ways.

A dissatisfied customer may:

- ✪ **Walk out of the facility**
- ✪ **Complain**
- ✪ **Shout**
- ✪ **Look unhappy**
- ✪ **Tell other people not to use the facility**

If the employees who have to deal with customers do not possess good communication and interpersonal skills, it can result in:

- ✪ **Rising complaints**
- ✪ **Loss of business**
- ✪ **Poor image**

Three things you should **always** do:

- ✪ **Stay calm; do not overreact by getting angry with the customer**

- ✪ **Listen carefully to why they are dissatisfied**

- ✪ **Concentrate on what they are saying and give them your undivided attention**

Three things you should **never** do:

- ✪ **Interrupt while they are telling you about their complaint**

- ✪ **Argue with the customer**

- ✪ **Offer something you have no authority to deliver**

  - **£100 refund**

  - **free holiday**

Offering extra services

As well as providing information, advice and staff who can deal with customers' problems, most facilities also provide extra services that are specific to their type of business. Here are some examples:

Selling goods

Some leisure and tourism facilities sell products to their customers (e.g. a museum may have a souvenir shop); others will allow businesses to set up on their premises (e.g. theme parks may encourage food outlets). This may attract visitors who want to shop as well as visit the theme park.

Coaching sessions

Quite often leisure facilities will offer some kind of training to their customers; this is known as coaching. Here are some examples:

- ✪ **Leisure centres that offer football classes to schoolchildren**

- ✪ **Swimming pools that offer sessions where customers can work towards their bronze medallion**

- ✪ **Skiing lessons at winter sports centres**

Activity 3.30

Contact your nearest leisure centre and find out what kind of coaching they offer.

Outdoor activities

Outdoor activities are very common and are offered by many leisure and tourism facilities. They include:

- ✪ **Rock climbing**

- ✪ **Guided walks**

- ✪ **Beach games**

- ✪ **Sightseeing**

- ✪ **Snowboarding**

- ✪ **Deep-sea diving**

Exercise 3.6

Find the following 10 outdoor activities hidden in the wordsearch. We have circled one of them for you.

Golf
Archery
Sailing
Rugby

Cricket
Gliding
Canoeing

Camping
Hiking
Fishing

C	A	N	O	E	I	N	G
R	A	A	B	D	C	E	N
I	R	M	G	H	F	I	I
C	C	J	P	K	L	F	D
K	H	M	N	I	I	L	I
E	E	O	P	S	N	O	L
T	R	Q	H	G	R	G	G
Y	Y	I	S	N	N	T	U
B	N	V	W	I	Y	Z	A
G	B	C	L	K	D	E	F
U	G	I	H	I	J	K	L
R	A	M	N	H	O	P	Q
S	R	S	T	U	X	W	V

Educational services

Many leisure and tourism facilities, including museums, theme parks and visitor centres, have started to put together packages for pupils, ranging from nursery and reception through to further and higher education. They include things like:

✪ **Worksheets and activities that can be completed when visiting a facility**

❂ **Films related to courses, such as a film about marketing a leisure and tourism facility**

❂ **Teacher preview days where teachers can check out a facility before they bring a group**

These extra services are often advertised in national newspapers aimed at teachers.

Activity 3.31

1   Ask your teacher for copies of newspapers which have educational sections (e.g. the *Times Educational Supplement*, the *Guardian*).

2   Find two advertisements about leisure and tourism facilities that offer educational services.

3   Contact the facilities and ask them to send you some information.

4   Share your information with others in your group and produce a display showing all the different information (you may even be able to persuade your teacher to take you to one of these facilities).

Food and drink

When customers visit leisure and tourism facilities they often expect food and drink. Some facilities only offer light snacks such as sandwiches, biscuits and drinks; others offer a full range of hot and cold meals.

Here are some examples of leisure and tourism facilities and the food and drink they offer:

● **Hotels** are often expected to offer breakfast, lunch, dinner and sometimes even a packed lunch. They need to cater for a range of dietary requirements (e.g. vegetarians). Larger hotels will also offer room service; they may have drinks cabinets in guest rooms and a hotel bar

Vending machines
machines that sell food and drink

● **Leisure centres** and swimming pools will have a snack bar and sometimes a larger cafe in addition to **vending machines**

● **Theme parks** will have lots of different cafes, restaurants and bars that offer food at a range of prices. They will also have fast-food facilities (e.g. hot dog stands and ice cream parlours)

Index

Key Words entries are bold: these pages show where the meaning of the word(s) is explained.